What the press is saying about John Woo ...

"The most famous member of a generation of directors known for over-the-top action, wild comedy, and sensual melodrama, John Woo's gone Hollywood without losing his Hong Kong roots."

—Entertainment Weekly

"Woo is such an action wizard that he can make planes or speedboats kick box, but his surprising strength this time is on a more human level. Diabolical cleverness shapes the way that John Travolta's nice guy and Nicolas Cage's sleek criminal trade faces. And trade lives . . . Beyond the bold strokes of casting these roles perfectly and creating a field day for his shrewd superstars, Woo accomplishes something near-impossible."

—New York Times, Face/Off review

"Woo, who became famous for his Hong Kong action pictures before hiring on in Hollywood, is a director overflowing with invention."

—Roger Ebert, Chicago Sun-Times

"And sometimes a gifted director can go beyond the conventional pleasures. With Face/Off, John Woo, the Hong Kong auteur (The Killer, Hard Boiled), has made his smartest, wildest, positively Woo-siest American thriller. Working from a vigorous script, Woo weaves his familiar touches— the slo-mo, the gleaming candles, the long coats flying in the breeze, the doves flying in a chapel as an omen of death— around the central fantasy of male bonding gone berserk."

—Time

D1225574

"Directed by John Woo, *Face/Off* is the most dazzling, eerie and evocative film of the year."

—San Francisco Chronicle

"John Woo is known for a cinema of violent delirium so breathtaking it plays like visual poetry, and *Face/Off*, though his third film in Hollywood, is the first to expose mainstream audiences to the master at his most anarchically persuasive. But, as those who've seen the director's cult favorite Hong Kong movies like *A Better Tomorrow*, *The Killer* and *Hard Boiled* can testify, Woo is also known for the sincerely sentimental underpinnings of his work. Bonding between men links all his films, which classically feature an emotional connection between the hero and the villain that's the strongest one on screen."

—Los Angeles Times

TEN THOUSAND BULLETS

Also by Christopher Heard

Dreaming Aloud: The Life and Films of James Cameron

TEN THOUSAND BULLETS

The Cinematic Journey of John Woo

Christopher Heard

lone eagle™
PUBLISHING COMPANY

Los Angeles

Ten Thousand Bullets: The Cinematic Journey of John Woo
Copyright © 2000 Christopher Heard

LONE EAGLE PUBLISHING COMPANY, LLC™
2301 Westwood Boulevard, Los Angeles, CA 90064
Tel: 800-FILMBKS • Fax: 310-471-4969
www.loneeagle.com and www.eaglei.com

Published by arrangement with Doubleday Canada
Printed in the United States of America
Cover photograph by Bryce Duffy
Cover design by Carla Green
Text design by Heather Hodgins

Library of Congress Cataloguing in Publication Data

Lone Eagle books may be purchased in bulk at special discounts for promotional or educational purposes. Special editions can be created to specifications. Inquiries for sales and distribution, textbook adoption, foreign language translation, editorial, and rights and permissions inquiries should be addressed to: Jeff Black, Lone Eagle Publishing, 2301 Westwood Boulevard, Los Angeles, CA 90064 or send e-mail to: info@loneeagle.com

Distributed to the trade by National Book Network, 800-462-6420
Lone Eagle Publishing Company is a registered trademark.

*For Mary, who taught me
what madly in love feels like.*

CONTENTS

ACKNOWLEDGMENTS

I have been very fortunate throughout the researching and writing of *Ten Thousand Bullets*. Many people gave willingly of their time and knowledge. Thanks must go first and foremost to my wonderful editor and friend Kathryn Exner. Her expertise and commitment are deeply appreciated. Thanks also to the terrific people at Doubleday who do a lot of work but rarely get any mention—Gloria Goodman, Christine Innes, Constance Mackenzie, Pam Robertson, Dara Rowland and Heather Hodgins. Thanks also to Don Sedgwick for getting behind this idea in the first place.

Thanks also to Chow Yun-Fat for generously giving me his time. To Mary Catherine Snelgrove of Columbia/Tri-Star Pictures for her help and organization. To writers Mike Werb and Michael Colleary for writing *Face/Off* and for giving me so many interesting stories. To Joel Greene for his swift responses.

The assistance of the following people also is appreciated—Heather McGillivray and Natalie Amaral at Twentieth Century Fox for putting me in a chair opposite John Woo for the first time and providing the initial spark for this book. Thanks also to Greg Ferris at Paramount for his support and kind words. To Colin Geddes and Julian Grant. To David Giammarco for his constant contributions and enthusiastic support. To Lorraine Clark at *MT: Movietelevision* for being terrific company during the long hours on the set of *Blackjack*. To Susan Smythe of Alliance/Atlantis Communications.

Special thanks to my good friends Ben Rotterman and John Foote, my partners on *Reel To Real*. Year after year we do what we love and love what we do.

Special thanks also to my father Bill Heard for including me in his long Sunday afternoon walks to movie theaters to catch matinees. My love for movies, movie history and movie culture can be traced directly to those times.

And lastly, thank you to the late David Overby. I never met Mr. Overby personally, but his excitement and championing of Hong Kong films, particularly the films of John Woo, first piqued my interest.

"I'm not a master; I'm just a hard-working filmmaker. I would like everyone to see me as a friend rather than a master."

JOHN WOO

PREFACE

One morning in the spring of 1989 I was sitting at my desk rewriting, for the sixth time, a horror screenplay called *Ringwood* because it had just been optioned by a producer who wanted some changes made. A friend of mine, the brilliant special-effects man Sean Sansom, had given me a videocassette that he insisted I watch because he knew that I would love it. It was an oddly titled movie from a Hong Kong director named John Woo. The movie was *A Better Tomorrow II* (1987). I knew nothing about Woo at the time and hadn't seen nor heard about the original *A Better Tomorrow* (1986).

I knew Sean's taste could be trusted, so I thought I would continue to write during the movie. As the movie unspooled I found myself looking up more and more until I wasn't looking back down at all. Within minutes I was transfixed. Sitting alone, I watched action sequences so dizzyingly frenetic that I found myself holding my breath until they were over. One sequence had two rival Hong Kong mobs in a gun battle at a luxurious estate. This gun battle was choreographed in such a way that you simply could not relax while it was going on. One gangster comes through a doorway with a gun in each hand. Another gangster from his mob sees him from across the room and yells, "Look out!" just as a rival gangster steps out from behind the door. The two rival thugs stand toe to toe and blast away at one another repeatedly until they are both riddled with bullets and still standing on pure adrenaline only. This sequence also made an impression on a most vociferous John Woo supporter, Quentin Tarantino, who wrote that very sequence from *A Better Tomorrow II* into his screenplay for *True Romance* (1993). You can see the sequence playing on the television in Clarence's (Christian Slater's) apartment.

I watched *A Better Tomorrow II* a couple of times and became increasingly fascinated by it. Sure, there were plenty of moves adapted from the cinematic canon of Sam Peckinpah, but Peckinpah received the same criticism himself. Peckinpah could be accused of "borrowing" or "paying homage" to Akira Kurosawa in several of his more memorable movies. What fascinated me was the familiar gangster genre as told by a filmmaker who was far removed from the culture that produced that genre.

I read up on Woo and found, to my astonishment, that he had also written and/or directed several kung-fu movies in the mid-seventies that I enjoyed as an adolescent. I sought out early Woo movies in Chinese video stores and my fascination grew.

In September 1989 I was thrilled to learn that Woo's newest film, *The Killer*, starring charismatic actor Chow Yun-Fat would be making its North American debut at the Toronto International Film Festival. After seeing it, I was convinced that Woo was re-inventing the action/gangster genre with a dash of his own visual poetry thrown in to make things really interesting.

Three years later, again at the Toronto International Festival of Festivals, Woo's wicked action movie, *Hard Boiled* debuted. It was at this same festival that avid John Woo fan Quentin Tarantino showed his feature film debut, *Reservoir Dogs*. During publicity interviews for his film, Tarantino, confessed that, after having seen John Woo's *A Better Tomorrow* he dressed like Chow Yun-Fat's character for weeks, wearing an identical trench coat and the same dark sunglasses. Tarantino further admitted that had it not been for the powerful influence of Woo's films, he might not have been at the festival with his own movie.

I have awaited and watched each new Woo film with relish. He is a fascinating filmmaker in that he projects none of the tough-guy characteristics that his movie protagonists possess.

The first opportunity I had to sit down with Woo took place in the Four Seasons Hotel in Beverly Hills in February 1995. He was promoting his second big Hollywood studio film, *Broken Arrow* (released in 1996), and consented to only four interviews. I was surprised by the humble way that Woo carries himself. When I tried to compliment him on his work he would redden and lower his eyes. I was fascinated by the dichotomous nature of this man. Could this polite, soft-spoken man be the same one who conjured the violent images I had been watching the past six years?

I am fascinated by the way that movies shape and define culture, and Woo is a particularly interesting example of this. *Ten Thousand Bullets: The Cinematic Journey of John Woo* shows that movies truly are a global language. American director Tarantino is influenced by Hong Kong director Woo. Woo was influenced by the French New Wave-gangster movies of Jean-Pierre Melville. Melville was influenced by the Hollywood gangster movies of the thirties and forties. It is all one big circle of inspiration and re-invention and, in the cinema culture of the eighties and nineties, Woo must be considered one of the most diverse and influential directors.

One

THE EARLY YEARS: LIGHT AT THE END OF A LONG, DARK TUNNEL

"With knowledge more, with virtue in store,
Our thrilling deeds will burst by the score,
All in your name,
All in good fame,
Delia echoes from shore to shore."
SCHOOL SONG, MATTEO RICCI COLLEGE, HONG KONG

Movie people are rewarded with riches, recognition and opportunities that go so far beyond the expectations of our normal lives, they can hardly be imagined. These people provide us with inspiration. They show us that anything is possible. They demonstrate that lofty dreams can be built over the flimsiest of foundations and can be attained no matter what your beginnings or your current status. No one is a better example of this, perhaps, than John Woo.

Woo was born Wu Yu-Sen in Guanchou, Canton Province, China in 1946. It is a large city, located south of the Pearl River with a population of about five million. The people of Guanchou believe their city was created by five celestial beings that came down from heaven on flying goats. In fact, the daily newspaper there is still called *The Flying Goat Times* (loosely translated).

In 1951, when the communists took over China, Woo's father, an unemployed philosophy professor, decided to move the family from Guanchou to Hong Kong. Life in Hong Kong was extremely tough for the Woo family. Their home was so small there was not enough room for everybody to sleep inside. Woo's father slept in the rain gutter in front of the dwelling, something that certainly caused and exacerbated his multiple illnesses. Much of the money the family earned was put towards treating back infections that plagued both his father, and Woo himself. When Woo was fifteen, his father died of tuberculosis—the affliction that had left him incapacitated and in and out of hospitals for ten years. The family's situation worsened when their shack burned to the ground, leaving them homeless in one of the roughest neighborhoods in Hong Kong—an area rife with drug dealers, prostitutes and street gangs.

The Woo family ended up living on the streets. Woo's mother worked at several menial jobs, sometimes more than one at a time. Eventually she was able to move the family into a small flat in the slums. There she continued to support Woo and his sister and brother.

Woo witnessed terrible violence throughout his childhood. Right outside his door, in fact. Clashes between the Communists and the Nationalists would result in huge gunfights leaving people shot and bleeding in the street. There were drug deals gone bad, prostitutes being beaten up. Rival gangs settling business. This all had quite an effect on the impressionable young boy.

"People were murdered right outside my door all the time. I saw it. I heard it. I felt like I was living in hell. I remember two big riots where people died right at our front door, killed by the police. Ever since then I wanted to use violence in my films to send a message. I do not chase violence for its own sake but for the beauty of the idea. I also think I need some kind of hero. The hero is ourselves, not just someone who kills the bad guys but someone who emphasizes how we might build up dignity."

The Woo family were devout Lutherans and lived close to a church. The church was a source of peace and comfort to them. When Woo was nine years old, an American family sponsored him through the church so he could attend school. He was so grateful for the assistance that he later seriously considered entering the priesthood himself as a way of repaying the kindness that he had received. He was ultimately refused entry into the priesthood because his thinking was deemed too "artistic" to be able to withstand the rigors and the discipline of that life. However, the church's influence is clear—you don't have to look very closely at Woo's films to notice that each is peppered with Christian iconography.

Even though he wasn't considered disciplined enough for the priesthood he was certainly subject to the strict regimen of his new Lutheran school. Woo remembers, "My school had one aim—that was to make decent young men and women of the slum dwellers. And I must say, that aim was certainly achieved."

As a child, Woo was painfully shy and self-conscious. He rarely spoke unless addressed and even then he had little to say. But he was dreaming. He started to dream early even though he had no idea how these dreams would manifest themselves.

An inquisitive child, he was interested in many things and embraced these interests with a passionate enthusiasm. "I loved painting and poetry and music. As a kid I wanted to be a musician, but as I grew up I knew I wouldn't be able to do all these things and devote equal amounts of time to all these hobbies." When Woo was just twelve years old, one of his teachers asked him, since he was showing great promise as an artist, to draw the cover page for the up coming Easter pageant program. Woo eagerly set about composing the picture and was quite proud of the results. His teachers, however, were taken aback by the finished piece. Woo had drawn a detailed face of Jesus. On top of Jesus' head was a crown of thorns. The shocking aspect of the picture was Jesus' pained expression and the blood cascading colorfully and profusely down his face. Woo, when asked why the picture was so gruesomely gory, calmly replied, "His pain must be seen to be understood."

It was during this time that Woo discovered movies, going to one almost every day, and they became a great source of joy and inspiration for him. Like most serious film fans, for him, a movie theater became a sort of sanc-tuary. He often spent afternoons and evenings sitting in a theater called the Alliance Française because that was the only cinema he knew of that showed foreign films. Woo's mother was also a serious film fan, introducing him to the American movies that would come to mean so much to him. Woo found himself drawn to such American films as *The Wizard of Oz* (1939), *Singin' in the Rain* (1952) and *West Side Story* (1961), films that transfixed him endlessly. "When I was a kid, I dreamed of a place with no hatred, where people loved each other and cared for each other. I could only find my dream in musicals." He remembers sitting in the darkened theater watching *The Wizard of Oz* in a euphoric state. "It was so beautiful I could hardly stand it. So colorful and magical." What particularly drew his attention were the people that populated these movies. "The people in them were so pretty and so elegant, so decent." Woo's father had neither time nor use for movies and Woo, remembers him saying that movies were fake. Woo, on the other hand, truly believed that movies are literally greater than reality.

Woo was about eleven years old when he knew he was a movie fan for life. "By that time I thought I was going crazy about movies. I used to draw characters like cowboys and warriors from the movies on plates of glass. Then I would cover myself with carpet like I was in the dark in a theater. I would light a torch and move it back and forth behind the glass and that projected these rudimentary images on the wall. So, you can see that I was something of a filmmaker even then."

Woo started to feel confined at the Lutheran junior high school he was attending, so he enrolled in Matteo Ricci College in Hong Kong, a liberal arts college named after a Jesuit priest. Matteo Ricci College looks like a hospital, or if you are particularly cynical, an above-ground multi-leveled parking garage. The school crest resembles a Maltese cross with an open book in the center. It is not an elite educational institution but it is where Woo matured as a young man. It is a place that afforded him great freedom of thought, where he started to tell himself, "Yes, I can do whatever I put my mind to." It was a place that gave him the sense that the Kowloon slums were behind him and would remain there if he applied himself to the tough task of making his dreams come true. As clichéd as that sounds, in Woo's case it happened to be true.

Woo was able to attend the college through the sponsorship of the American family that aided him earlier in his education. Woo was a good student when he applied himself. He had an excellent aptitude for the arts and the idea of learning was very exciting to him. But once he discovered cinema his schooling began to suffer. He wanted desperately to learn about every aspect of movie-making, but those lessons were not to be found in class. He ended up skipping class after class, day after day, preferring to spend time in movie theaters, art galleries and libraries.

When he was sixteen years old, Woo left school for good, not by choice but due to the recent death of his father. He immediately took a job with a newspaper called *The Chinese Student Weekly*. He found himself hanging around with several students who were also associated with the news-paper and soon joined the The Chinese Student Weekly Theatre Company where he tried his hand at acting. It is certainly not without precedent that a writer, director or producer should come to his profession after trying acting. Mega-producer Robert Evans (*Love Story* [1970], *The Godfather* [1972]) was an actor throughout the fifties before turning to producing. Academy Award-winning director Sir Richard Attenborough was a respected actor before he turned his attention to directing (although he was lured back before the cameras by Steven Spielberg to co-star in both *Jurassic Park* movies). For Woo, getting on stage and acting meant freedom—the freedom to express himself in an arena that would ensure he was being listened to. Woo started gaining the greater self-confidence and sense of power that creativity can bring. He even joined a ballroom dancing class and became fairly good at it. But it was the movies that continued to occupy the young man's attention.

Woo found solace in the darkened movie theaters he was spending so much time in, only now, these films he watched, these images he was seeing, were inspiring him, making him think that he might like to become a part of this world some day. Some of the students at *The Chinese Student Weekly* had an informal film appreciation society. They would go to the movies and then convene in groups to discuss them and to educate themselves. Woo's interests soon shifted from the flighty musicals that had provided the escapism he so desperately desired as a young boy to the works of directors like Francois Truffaut, Michelangelo Antonioni, Ingmar Bergman and Jean-Pierre Melville. Melville in particular was a favorite of the young Woo, especially Melville's noir classic, the down-and-dirty *Le Samourai* (1967), a film that Woo still raves about as among his all-time favorites.

Woo is very open about this point in his life because he feels that the person he is was shaped at that particular time.

"The boss at the newspaper was a very kind man who made the paper's offices available as a sort of art center," says Woo. "There were several people who had different artistic interests, and would form little groups within the newspaper—there was a poetry group, an art group, a philosophy group; I met up with the group of people who loved film. The newspaper rented art films for us to watch and afterwards we would discuss them. That was right around the time I started stealing theory books to study with."

Woo decided to take a shot at making movies himself rather than spending a lifetime watching movies made by others. He set out to learn everything he possibly could about the movies, both historically and in terms of the basic technical knowledge that he wanted to commit to memory before peering through his first viewfinder. Woo decided that the only way he could learn what he needed to know (aside from the student film discussions) was through books. He scoured the libraries and bookstores for anything and everything he could find on the subject of films and film theory, often "borrowing" the volumes from the bookstores so he could study them at his leisure.

In 1966, at the age of twenty, Woo made the leap and started filming his own little epics. Over the next two years, he made as many of these little 8 mm and 16 mm movies as he could. All of these early efforts have been lost, which is unfortunate. It would be interesting indeed to watch the minor-league efforts of a talent like Woo;

often the early efforts of major filmmakers show clearly where the roots of their passion lie.

Another thing to consider when looking at the development and success of a filmmaker is timing. Woo had the talent and the passion but he was also in Hong Kong where the film industry was about to expand like never before. A young Chinese actor named Bruce Lee was about to return to Hong Kong to star in a movie that would stand the action genre film on its ear, making him an internationally recognized star. And young Woo was about to take his little films to the legendary Cathay Studios looking for any kind of entrée.

Two

1969–1973: WOO GETS A FOOT IN THE DOOR

"When I stepped into the studio for the first time I couldn't believe where I was. I had so many ideas I was almost bursting."

JOHN WOO

Woo's period of self-discovery as an amateur filmmaker during 1964 brought him to the front gates of Cathay Studios in Hong Kong, where he impressed people enough to be given the position of general apprentice and script assistant. He fell in love with the energy of a working film studio but was quickly frustrated by his role within it. His desire to make movies was so strong it became difficult to watch other people living his dream.

Cathay Studios were originally based in Singapore and were run by an enterprising man named Loke Wan-Tho. Looking to expand into the hugely lucrative Mandarin film market, Wan-Tho bought the Hong Kong-based Yonghua Studios in 1955. Yonghua was going through its latest of many financial difficulties, allowing the business-man to buy it relatively cheaply. Won-tho restructured the Yonghua studio, giving it the rather uninspired name of MP and GI Studios (meaning Motion Picture and General Investment). Numerous comedies and romances were made for the Mandarin market and the studio earned a reputation for creating quality movies compara-ble to those made in the industrialized atmosphere of top Hollywood movie studios. For several years, Won-tho's name and the MP and GI symbol were synonymous with quality Mandarin moviemaking. Their movies had a sophistication that Mandarin films of past eras did not.

In 1964 Wan-Tho was killed in a plane crash in Taiwan. The MP and GI studios were officially renamed Cathay Studios in his honor. Without the guiding hand of Wan-Tho there was a noticeable depreciation in the stan-dards of filmmaking at Cathay.

By the time Woo joined Cathay, the studio was all but going through the motions.

Woo's early work at the studio consisted of helping to dress sets and acting as a general helper. Dressing sets initially interested him. He could hang around the set as movies were being made, absorbing even more of the craft of making films. After several months of this, however, Woo started feeling that if he was to get anywhere in this business he would need to show that he had something to contribute other than carrying props. He became consumed with the thought that he could create better movies than the ones he was helping to make. Woo would spend time hanging around the director's chair when he could, insinuating himself into conversations involving the script or the action. Often his suggestions were rebuked but every once in a while someone would look at him and say "good idea."

Woo, like everyone else, could sense that Cathay was on the downhill slide. He kept his ear to the ground, looking for someone or someplace that might allow him more experience than he was getting at Cathay. That opportunity eventually came from the other big Hong Kong moviemaker—the Shaw Brothers Studio. Woo was offered a job at Shaw Brothers Studio as an assistant director with the promise of a shot, some day, at writing and directing his own movie—provided he was willing to work hard and be patient. Having worked as a gofer at Cathay for almost two years, he saw this proposal as one he could not refuse.

• • •

Sir Run Run Shaw and his three brothers, sons of a wealthy Shanghai textile factory owner, founded the Shaw Brothers Studio. Shaw Brothers built a post-war empire that included the production, distribution and exhibition of movies all across Asia. In the early days, the studio was run as a feudal-type operation in that the stars, known and loved all over Asia, often lived in dormitories and were paid next to nothing. They had no say over which directors or actors they worked with or which films they would appear in.

In 1970, Raymond Chow, an upstart movie producer who came up through the ranks with Shaw Brothers, quit and bought the rapidly disintegrating Cathay Studios. He renamed Cathay Studios after his own production company and called the whole outfit Golden Harvest. Chow changed the studio's traditional factory-like style of film-making, making it more a central location for independent-style films and filmmakers. Golden Harvest would quickly become one of the most successful movie production companies in the world. However, many believe that the dissolution of Cathay Studios brought about the death of the studio system in the Hong Kong film industry.

Once Chow set up Golden Harvest, Shaw Brothers found that it suddenly had some stiff competition. Chow seemed to be able to tap into talent that would cross over into international acceptance (like Bruce Lee and Jackie

Chan). But Shaw Brothers responded to the challenge, and many of the films that made the Hong Kong film industry as explosive as it was for a couple of decades carried the Shaw Brothers name.

(By the mid-eighties, when the kung-fu movie craze had died down and when independent films had all but cornered the Asian market, Shaw Brothers started to relax. Run Run Shaw was knighted by the Queen and founded the Shaw University in Hong Kong. Brother Runme Shaw went to Singapore to oversee the family business there. Then Shaw Brothers suddenly abandoned the film industry altogether and founded Hong Kong TVB, now the major supplier of television soap operas in Hong Kong, where several Hong Kong movie stars got their start.)

One of the more successful directors working out of the Shaw Brothers Studio at the time was Chang Cheh. Cheh gave North America its first taste of flat-out "kung-fu" movies, movies that became very popular in North America for a few years before retreating to Hong Kong (a trend that started right after the death of the charismatic Bruce Lee in 1973). Cheh's *Five Fingers of Death* (1970) was a bizarre and exotic action movie that features men with super-human skills and a seemingly limitless tolerance for violence and physical pain. It's a carnival of eye-gouging, disemboweling, hands being pushed into burning sand—all sorts of creative violence in a movie in which the action begins at the opening credits and continues through the final credits. Cheh would also make what some consider to be the quintessential kung-fu movie of the era, *Five Deadly Venoms* (1979). *Five Deadly Venoms* is an unbelievably wild tale of friendship, greed and betrayal and it was the first of a very successful series of Shaw Brothers kung-fu epics that all featured the same five actors.

Woo worked closely with Cheh on several films as his assistant director. It was this exposure to the great action director that would prove to be the greatest professional influence in Woo's career. He not only patterned himself after Cheh thematically but also his behavior as a director was greatly influenced by the elder filmmaker. On a Woo set the director is the boss but everyone else on the project is treated with respect and courtesy. For Cheh's part the respect was mutual, and he helped guide Woo along. Cheh knew that Woo was marking time before becoming a writer and director just as he had when starting out.

Cheh began his career as a scriptwriter in Shanghai. In 1962, he joined the Shaw Brothers Studio in the same capacity. He was made their chief scriptwriter with the promise that one day he would be allowed to direct a movie himself. That promise was quickly kept when Shaw Brothers realized how prolific Cheh was and how popular his stories were. Cheh was given the opportunity to direct several swordplay movies throughout the late sixties that were enormously successful. Many of these movies were made with Woo acting as his assistant. Woo contributed ideas when his enthusiasm got the better of him, but mostly he watched the older director, soaking up his techniques with regard to the timing and staging of physical action scenes. He was also made aware of the importance of including strong themes within an action movie, elevating it to something more than what it appears to be on the surface.

Cheh is now recognized as one of the true innovators in the history of Hong Kong cinema. Before Cheh, Hong Kong action movies were often shot in black and white and depicted martial arts in a respectful, almost spiritual manner. Cheh made his movies with a garishly colorful palate using broadly sketched brush strokes. That particular imprint is evident in John Woo's *Hard Boiled* (1992).

When asked about his influences Woo will often mention Jean-Pierre Melville or Sam Peckinpah. If probed further he always talks about Cheh as the man who taught him what it was to be a professional filmmaker. Cheh also provided young Woo with the powerful guidance a mentor can provide. Woo's father did not care for cinema and died before he could provide any moral support or encouragement. In Cheh, Woo could look up to a man who started out just like he did and made his dreams come true. Cheh provided Woo with a living example of the possibilities granted by hard work and perseverance.

Cheh would go on to create seventy movies in just fifteen years, making him the most prolific filmmaker to come out of the Shaw Brothers Studio. Bey Logan writes in his book *Hong Kong Action Cinema*, "It is the raw power of the central male performances, together with the extravagance of the protracted combat sequences, that raises the best of [Cheh's] work above the general standard of Shaw's output."

Woo was itching to expand his horizons. Working in such close proximity to Cheh made him want to get behind the camera himself sooner rather than later. He started hinting that he was ready to do some directing if someone was willing to give him the opportunity. He would jump at the chance to direct some second-unit stuff here or an action sequence there. As enthusiastic as he was, he was not entirely optimistic that his promised shot at directing would happen any time soon. In the Hong Kong film industry of the early seventies a "young" director would be in his forties and it was virtually unheard of that a kid in his twenties would be given the responsibility of directing a movie. But in 1973, Woo was given the break he had been waiting for. His close friend had just made a surprise financial killing and was interested in investing some of the money in the film industry. Arrangements were made for Woo to write and direct his first feature film.

The result was a martial-arts movie called *The Young Dragons* (1973). Though hardly potential Oscar material, Woo is still very proud of *The Young Dragons* for the simple reason that "*The Young Dragons* made me one of the youngest directors ever in Hong Kong." Woo hired an eager, ambitious young fight choreographer named Jackie Chan to design some of his fight sequences. The film would also mark Woo's first brush with censorship. *The Young Dragons* was considered so violent that it was shelved for a while. The censors seemed most offended by one particular aspect of the movie. Woo had had a special glove designed for the bad guy to wear, a glove that was covered in nails and razor blades. When the bad guy struck people with his glove, the victim bled profusely. The censors were disturbed not so much by the amount of bloodshed, but rather by the potential risk that kids would go out and try to concoct their own versions of the glove and imitate the behavior of the bad guy.

Despite this, the movie was seen to be interesting and commercial enough to capture the attention of Golden Harvest, the emerging film studio that had recently hit it big with the wildly successful Bruce Lee movies, including *The Big Boss* (1971—called *Fists of Fury* in North America). These movies had, surprisingly, gone on to make a fortune overseas and made an international star out of Bruce Lee. Golden Harvest decided to distribute *The Young Dragons*. They were happy enough with the results, both artistic and financial, to offer young Woo a contract to write and direct films exclusively for them. Woo was ecstatic at the offer. He was not happy about leaving Shaw Brothers and the influence of Cheh but he had to look towards his future. Woo now looked in the mirror and told himself, "I am now a filmmaker." The idea filled him with pride but also with a sense of anxiety—he had so many stories he wanted to tell and so many cinematic journeys he wanted to take. Now, having gotten *both* feet in the door, it was up to him to remain on the inside.

Three

1974–1985:
WOO BECOMES A
FILMMAKER

*"My movies of this period were all very
exaggerated, pretty much like cartoons.
They were like Mel Brooks-style movies."*

JOHN WOO

Now working as a director for Golden Harvest, John
Woo worked hard to gain as much experience as quickly
as possible. He wisely followed up *The Young Dragons* with
two similar movies, *The Dragon Tamers* (1974) and *Hand
of Death* (1974). They were both low-budget films, shot in
Korea. He was encouraged that his bosses at Golden

Harvest trusted him, neophyte that he still was, at the helm of a couple of movies shot in another country. He was also happy about being given the responsibility for two movies that Golden Harvest thought would be quick money-makers for them. The fact that these two movies were shot in Korea, removed somewhat from his overseers, meant that Woo was able to make changes to the flat-out action scripts, putting his own spin on them. When he speaks of *The Dragon Tamers* and *Hand of Death* it is with fondness. "What I liked about those two movies was the fact that even though they were action movies, the main thing about them was their love stories." Before directing his first big hit for the studio, he made *Hand of Death*, a routine martial-arts movie that would have disappeared quickly from the collective memories of movie fans had it not been for the presence of an eager young martial-arts actor named Jackie Chan.

Chan's success is staggering. These days he commands upwards of $20 million per picture and collects a healthy percentage of the sizable profits his movies make worldwide. Yet he was born to a family so poor they thought seriously about selling him to the British doctor who delivered him. When Chan was a young child, his father turned him over to the China Drama Academy boarding school where children were trained in the art of Peking Opera, a combination of martial arts, acrobatics, mime, swordplay and singing. The Peking Opera was reputed to be a brutalizing experience, both physically and mentally. Beatings and starvation as a method of punishment were commonplace. It has been suggested that part of Chan's incredible stunt ability stems from his Peking Opera training and the likelihood that his tolerance for pain was established when he was a young boy. During his ten long years at the school he rarely underwent any academic schooling, as the other disciplines were considered much more important. When he left the Peking Opera in 1971 at the age of seventeen, he was a well-trained martial artist. A fellow former Peking Opera student, Sammo Hung, was making a name for himself in movies as a stunt performer and coordinator. Chan asked Hung, or "Big Brother" as he was known at school, if there was any stunt work he might be hired for.

Hung, sympathetic to the plight of his "Little Brother," directed him to the busiest Hong Kong movie studio at the time, the Shaw Brothers Studio, where Chan was promptly hired as a menial laborer and part-time stuntman.

It's been said that Woo gave Chan his first break in film. However, Chan starred in a movie a year earlier called *Little Tiger of Canton* (1971). Chan had been working as a stuntman until this point and wanted desperately to make the step up to acting. The film was not successful and Chan, completely disheartened, believed his shot at stardom had been wasted. Broke and despondent, he headed to Australia where his parents were living. Chan worked as a painter and a mason by day and a dishwasher by night, but his dreams of being a movie actor persisted. He returned to Hong Kong for one last shot at success.

In his 1998 autobiography *I am Jackie Chan: My Life in Action* Chan described how he came to be cast in Woo's *Hand of Death*. During a slow period, Chan called Hung to see if there was any work around. Coincidentally, Hung had just been hired as stunt coordinator on *Hand of Death*, and told Chan that he would put in a good word for him with the director. "Who's the director?" asked Chan. "Some new guy—never heard of him, his name is Woo," replied Hung.

Chan was hired as a stuntman on the recommendation of "Big Brother" and reported to the set. He was shocked and delighted when Woo decided to cast him in a co-starring role. Woo says he saw an enthusiasm and a freshness in Chan that was just what he was looking for. He was also impressed with Chan's fearless approach to stunt work.

The experience of working with Woo and making *Hand of Death* was a good one. "John Woo was different than the other directors I had worked with," says Chan. "He really knew what he was doing. He cared about every move, every stunt, every fight, as if he was performing them himself. He was very kind and treated us all very well."

When asked about Woo, Chan smiles broadly and speaks of Woo as a compadre, like a fellow struggler who made good. He says that even though Woo did not give him his first role (as the popular Asian movie myth goes), Woo did give him a platform in *Hand of Death* without which he never would have been noticed. Chan says he would love to have the opportunity to work with Woo again but doesn't really see that as a reasonable expectation given that they both are very successful and are on quite diverse career paths. But they do run into one another every now and then in Hollywood. On these occasions, says Chan, he always pauses to consider the fact that two poor Chinese kids have made it to the very top of the Hollywood A-list. Both have achieved things that neither would have dared dream about as kids.

Woo's martial-arts movies were becoming known for their style. Most martial-arts movies of the day featured several chaotic, drawn-out combat scenes that involved the hero fighting legions of attackers. Woo, however, staged well-thought-out fight scenes involving only two fighters squaring off and pitting their very different skills against one another. And *Hand of Death* contained several Woo-isms that would make him legendary later on. His action scenes were set against a backdrop of symbolic gestures of loyalty and brotherhood among men fighting for a common cause. *Hand of Death* features a former Shaolin Temple monk named Chow Cher Fen (James Tien) who has betrayed his holy roots and become a Manchu commander controlling a Chinese province through oppression. The Buddhist monks at the Shaolin Temple order their finest kung-fu fighter Yun Fe (Dorian Tan) to seek out and destroy the villain. Yun meets a long-haired youth on his journey, played by Chan, who is also an excellent fighter, and enlists his help. There is a huge climatic battle that ends with the heroes conquering the oppressor and the wayward long-haired youth learning lessons about courage and loyalty.

Hand of Death was not a success either financially or critically, and Chan was again left without any immediate prospects. He was so discouraged he returned to Australia and his family for what he thought was for good, deciding that movie stardom was simply beyond his grasp. He would probably have stayed there, toiling as a manual laborer, had fate not intervened. Chan received a call from Lo Wei's production company, maker of the early Bruce Lee movies. They were searching for someone who could be "the new Bruce Lee." They had seen Chan in Woo's *Hand of Death* and were impressed enough to seek him out.

John Woo came along at precisely the right time. By the mid-seventies the Hong Kong film industry was starting to change, moving away from the kind of action movies that Woo cut his teeth on, to a more stylized, diverse cinema that was exactly what he dreamed of doing.

In the early seventies, North American audiences became fascinated by Asian martial arts, and movie theaters were suddenly showing kung-fu movies titled *Five Fingers of Death* (1970), *Duel of the Iron Fist* (1969), *Beach of the War Gods* (1971) and *Chinese Hercules* (1974). Perhaps the first true genius of the time was a young Chinese immigrant actor named Bruce Lee. Lee had wowed North American TV audiences in the late sixties with his lightning fast martial-arts moves in a short-lived but still-syndicated show called *The Green Hornet*, in which he was cast as Kato, sidekick and chauffeur to millionaire publisher and crime fighter Britt Reid, also known as The Green Hornet. Although Lee was on camera for only a few minutes each episode he was the one who got all the fan mail and was asked to make all the personal appearances. Lee realized there was significant interest in the exotic arts from the Far East and decided to heighten his own profile by developing a series in which he would play a former Chinese monk, skilled to an almost mythical level in the martial arts, who roams the American west at the turn of the century. ABC loved the idea and produced the series but the crestfallen Lee was told that he was "too Asian" to play the character called Kwai Chang Caine and that American audiences would not accept an Asian hero in a TV series. David Carradine would play the role, while Lee headed back to Hong Kong to star in a couple of movies that would bring about a new film genre—the kung-fu movie.

Lee's first movie was shot in Thailand for Shaw Brothers and the upstart Golden Harvest companies. *The*

Big Boss (1971—called *Fists of Fury* in North America) went on to fill theaters the world over. A charismatic new movie star with extraordinarily unique skills was born. Lee enjoyed the limelight and dreamt of the kind of global movie-star status enjoyed by some of the actors to whom he taught martial arts, like Steve McQueen and James Garner. He followed his debut with an even greater success, *The Chinese Connection* (1972—oddly, called *Fists of Fury* in Asia).

By now every theater owner wanted to show kung-fu films, and the Hong Kong film industry responded by pumping out as many of them as they could. Woo benefited by this gold rush in the first few films of his career but he but he never lost sight of his goal. For now, he was simply producing product to be shipped anywhere there was a demand for another kung-fu movie.

Hollywood, the place where Lee's dreams had been trampled only a couple years earlier, now came knocking. Lee accepted an offer to star in a movie called *Enter the Dragon* (1973) for producer Jerry Weintraub and Warner Brothers. *Enter the Dragon* was a martial-arts movie with touches of James Bond thrown in to make it more accessible to the North American market. The result was a phenomenal international success. *Enter the Dragon* became the highest-grossing movie in Hong Kong's history (until that record was broken by Woo's *A Better Tomorrow* [1986]). A by-product of that success was an offer to Lee from the high-profile movie producer Joseph E. Levine that would make Lee the highest-paid actor on earth.

Lee honored his commitment to Golden Harvest to write, direct and star in a couple of movies for them before moving back to the United States to fulfill his lucrative American deal. The first movie was *The Way of the Dragon* (1972—released in North America as *Return of the Dragon*), starring Lee and Chuck Norris. It was also a huge hit, demonstrating that Lee had talent as a director as well. He moved quickly to write, direct and star in his next Hong Kong movie, an eccentric martial-arts adventure called *Game of Death*, but tragically he would not live to finish the movie that was about one-quarter completed. On July 20, 1973, Lee died suddenly in Hong Kong at the age of thirty-two, having suffered a brain edema caused by an allergic reaction to pain medication taken for a headache. The doctor who performed the autopsy on Lee remarked that he had kept himself in such good shape that he had the body of an eighteen-year-old. After Lee died, the Hong Kong film industry slumped because it no longer had an internationally recognized Asian actor who was also a legitimately talented writer and director. Martial-arts movies were still being made, but without the drawing power of Lee, the mystique faded fast. Asian producers, writers and directors had to evolve or they would cease to exist. This was exactly the shift in the industry that Woo had been hoping for—the opportunity to make movies based on his own ideas rather than one martial-arts action movie after another.

After *Hand of Death*, Woo made a movie that was a departure for him, a comedic Cantonese Opera film called *Princess Chang Ping* (1975). Even though he immensely enjoyed being a real film director, he still yearned for that seemingly elusive opportunity to make a movie that was distinctly his own—something he conceived, wrote and directed himself. "When I was making *Princess Chang Ping*," he says, "I started to dream about making *A Better Tomorrow*, but the producers insisted that I stick with comedies even though I didn't think I was suited to them."

Princess Chang Ping was a hit and had producers starting to look at Woo as one of the brightest new talents on the scene.

Next, he served as a production designer on a film called *The Private Eyes* (1976), following that with a B-movie called *Pilferer's Progress* (1977)—also known as *Money Crazy*—a screwball-type comedy. Both of these movies performed well at the box office.

Hong Kong newspaper profiles started describing him as the "new golden boy of Hong Kong film comedies."

In 1977, he made *Last Hurrah for Chivalry*. This was a standard kung-fu movie that he made only because it was suggested rather strongly to him that he make it. To be fair, some of the martial-arts sequences in *Last Hurrah for Chivalry* are quite good, but the movie in general is standard for the genre. In this movie, Woo allowed himself the luxury of experimentation. "I combined the theatricality of period drama with modern dialogue in the writing of the story about friendship and chivalry. Historical figures, such as Jin Key (who attempted to assassinate the Emperor of Qin) were my heroes, since they were willing to die for their beliefs." The story was your basic lone warrior with mystical fighting skills up against legions of bad guys.

Amidst all the silliness there is one truly eccentric sequence that is worthy of note. The hero of the movie, played by Wei Pei, has an extended fight scene with someone known as the "sleeping wizard," a martial-arts master who fights while asleep!

Woo went right to work on his next movie called *From Rags to Riches* (1977). Woo considers it one of his favorites simply because he was finally allowed some real freedom. "I filmed it exactly the way I wanted, using a lot of close-ups. I think I am good at creating a gallery of minor characters, which this film has a lot of, and I was able to create a sharp satire on different types of people thrown together in the same environment."

Feeling as though he'd arrived, and confident that he had a future in the movie industry, Woo asked the woman he loved to marry him. Annie Ngau Chun-lung accepted and they were married in 1978. A year later, the couple celebrated the birth of their first child, a girl they named Kimberley.

As Woo grew comfortable with the fact that he was now a bona fide filmmaker, he yearned to make his own movies—movies through which he could apply his cinematic knowledge and inspiration. His employers at Golden Harvest were dumbfounded to hear him talk of wanting to make movies like *The Wild Bunch* and *Bonnie and Clyde*, given his apparent talent at making comedies. Woo spoke of his love for movies like Henri Clouzot's 1953 French movie *The Wages of Fear*, explaining to his employers that this was the sort of film he hoped to direct. *The Wages of Fear* (expertly remade in 1977 by William Friedkin as *Sorcerer*) is a fabulous movie about four criminals hiding out in a small jungle town in South America. An oil company nearby needs four volunteers for a suicide mission that involves driving trucks loaded with nitroglycerine 200 miles into the jungle where it is needed to blow out an oil-well fire. *The Wages of Fear* features everything that Woo loves in a movie—loyalty, danger, betrayal and triumph through the sheer force of will. In production meetings, however, Golden Harvest would urge him to make movies that appealed to the lowest common denominator.

In 1980, Woo decided to leave Golden Harvest. He was still under contract, but his arrangement with Golden

Harvest was in its final months. He headed to Los Angeles with his family to take a look around. He had no real intention of working there, but it was where the movies he loved were made. It was in Los Angeles that the Woos' second daughter was born. They named the baby Angeles after her birthplace.

A couple of months later, Woo returned to Hong Kong. He headed for the newly formed, more progressive Cinema City. Cinema City was an independent studio founded by Karl Maka, Raymond Wong and comedian Dean Shek—all actors, directors and producers. Cinema City made its money on family-oriented, formulaic films. Since Woo had carved a niche for himself in comedies, they assumed he would be perfect for the kind of work they were doing. It was not what Woo wanted, but he had a family to support and he needed the work. He was disappointed by the fact that he had left Golden Harvest for the momentum of a fresh new company only to find himself right back where he started. Woo was left to his own devices to create films for Cinema City, but they had to fall within the parameters of what the company considered fast and profitable. Woo quickly ran out of formulaic ideas, and the ones he did come up with were rejected by the bosses. Cinema City evaluated the situation and sent him to Taiwan, ostensibly to work in the business office. Whether this was a form of punishment for his lack of output, or whether they were simply trying to keep him employed during the dry spell is uncertain, but Woo wasn't ready to give up directing.

In 1981 Woo did manage to direct a comedy called *Laughing Times*, starring comedian and Cinema City partner Shek. One condition of making the movie was that Woo be credited under a pseudonym as he was still technically under contract to Golden Harvest for another few months and was not to direct a movie for any other company during that time.

After he was free of his Golden Harvest contract, he did manage to make films at the Cinema City facilities in Taiwan. He worked steadily and was somewhat relieved to be directing, but these films were still not what he wanted to be producing.

In 1981, Woo made and co-starred in what many would consider to be the most bizarre film in his long and diverse filmography. It was called *To Hell With the Devil*, resembling both *Faust* by Goethe and the Dudley Moore/Peter Cook Faustian send-up *Bedazzled* (1967).

In the Woo version, the spirit of a defrocked priest and a cohort of Satan duke it out, with the winner receiving possession of the soul of an aspiring pop singer. A character named Flit, the devil's assistant, challenges the priest as they are on their way to their respective hereafters. Into this sequence, Woo pours all his Christian stereotypes. Heaven is a place in the clouds where everyone smiles and wears white flowing robes. Hell is filled with fire and brimstone. God looks like Mark Twain and Satan looks like German actor Max Shreck. Woo is, above all else, a movie fan, and *To Hell With the Devil* is peppered with references to *Gone With the Wind* (1939), *The Exorcist* (1973) and *Close Encounters of the Third Kind* (1977). There's even an homage to the old Hammer studios in England, and their film *The Horror of Dracula* (1958).

There are some interesting special effects in *To Hell With the Devil* but the story line is silly and nothing in the movie really works dramatically.

To Hell With the Devil also contains some of the most unintentionally hilarious dialogue Woo has ever included in his movies, including the following notable examples: "What you need is a canned woman." "What is a soul? It's just toilet paper." "He's a camel but you don't have to walk a mile for him."

Growing ever more despondent, Woo started drinking heavily. He was desperate for a change, for fate to intervene and provide a change of direction. Woo continued to direct but the outcome of his work suggests that Cinema City's decision to send him to Taiwan to make movies was precisely the wrong thing to do.

In 1984, his inspiration clearly waning, he made *Plain Jane to the Rescue*, which is perhaps one of the worst movies he has ever made. To date this is the only John Woo movie with a female star and main character and it's fairly obvious that he wrestled with the film. He followed this with another terrible movie, *Run Tiger Run*, a silly comedy about a little brat who is adopted by his rich grandparents after his own parents die. There is a big-hearted nanny in the story who tries to teach the poor misunderstood little boy the wonder of life.

During this period another filmmaker was making waves in Hong Kong, a filmmaker who would act as the hand of fate that Woo sought.

Tsui Hark, born Tsui Man-kong, changed his name to Hark (meaning "to overcome") after being teased about his name while attending school in Texas ("the other students called me King Kong"). He began his filmmaking career in Hong Kong at the age of 27, when he made back-to-back movies that were met with general indifference (*The Butterfly Murders* in 1979 and *We're Going to Eat You* in 1980). But his second movie of 1980, *Dangerous Encounters of the First Kind*, really put him on the map, but for the wrong reasons. A movie of stultifying nihilism and violence, it concerns three teenage boys who plant a bomb in a theater for fun. This act gains them the attention of a bizarre woman who coerces them into engaging in larger acts of terrorism. The movie ends with mercenaries hunting the four of them down and killing them all. When the movie was released (it was titled *Don't Play With Fire* in some markets) many thought, indeed hoped, that Hark would never make another film.

Dean Shek Raymond Chow and Karl Maka decided to put the resources of Cinema City behind a fourth Hark movie. The decision was odd in that Hark was making movies that were diametrically opposed to Cinema City movies. Tsui surprised everyone by making a movie called *All the Wrong Clues . . . For All the Right Solutions*, a gangster spoof that was a popular hit and earned Hark the Golden Horse Award for Best Director of 1981 (the Taiwanese equivalent of an Academy Award).

In 1984 after making a movie called *Aces Go Places III*, a James Bond send-up that went on to earn huge profits for Cinema City, Hark decided to make a change. He was restless and saw that he had the opportunity to expand his horizons. In April 1984, Tsui Hark and his wife, Nan Sun Shi, founded their own company called Film Workshop. At the same time, Woo was losing his battle with his drinking problem.

Nan Sun Shi remembers, "John and my husband would go out drinking, telling stories and pouring their hearts out to each other." Woo confessed that he no longer had the drive or the motivation to make the kind of movies that he was expected to make for Cinema City, that he wanted desperately to make a gangster movie.

Fortunately, by the end of 1984, Woo had made a movie that solidly proved his talents as a director and provided him with material that was up to his standards. *Time You Need a Friend* is a delightful comedy that is a Hong

Kong version of the Neil Simon hit play *The Sunshine Boys* (which later became an Oscar-winning film). In Simon's play two long-since-retired vaudevillians are lured out of retirement one last time to do a TV special.

Woo's version features the wonderfully expressive actors Ren Ren and Shien Bien as former comedians who haven't spoken to each other in fourteen years. They find themselves hosting a telethon as a result of some covert maneuvering by the show's producers. During the telethon they go from being at each other's throats to returning to the deep friendship they had shared throughout most of their lives. In a rather bizarre about-face, the movie ends with Shien dying of a heart attack while the appreciative audience applauds him wildly for the work he has done on the telethon.

Later that year, Hark invited Woo to return to Hong Kong to write and direct a gangster movie about a young police cadet and his triad (organized crime gang) brother. Woo would finally have the chance to make the film he had always wanted to make. Hark, for the first time in his career, would set up and produce a movie that someone else would direct.

Their efforts would create a movie that would change the way Hong Kong films were perceived internationally, make a huge star out of a Hong Kong soap-opera actor and change forever Woo's life.

Four

1986–1988:
A NEW DAWN AND A
BETTER TOMORROW

"Sometimes I'm shooting an action sequence and I relate to it. I get very emotional. I relate to what is happening in the real world. For example, if I'm shooting a scene where the hero is fighting bad guys and I've heard on the radio about some little child getting murdered by some maniac I get very angry. I get pretty upset. And bring that to the scene. I look at the bad guy as the murderer and I'm thinking, let's beat him harder, let's hit him with more bullets."

JOHN WOO

Rarely can an artist on a distinct career path bring about abrupt change in his work and go on to even greater success in the second incarnation. But it has been done. Novelist Elmore Leonard toiled as a writer of western novels in relative obscurity until he turned his attentions to crime writing. He then set his tales on the mean streets of Detroit and Miami and started generating some of the best contemporary crime fiction ever written.

Woo also belongs in this company. Despite the variety in his work, until 1986, one might have concluded that Woo was a journeyman director, with a flair for comedy. He had certainly made a name for himself as a director but, whenever asked about his success, he always threw in an addendum: "What I would really like to do is a gangster movie, like French director Jean-Pierre Melville."

In 1967, French director Jean-Pierre Melville made *Le Samourai*, one in a series of three French gangster movies. This terrific little movie, starring Alain Delon and Francoise Perier, delved deeply into the rituals and thoughts of criminals. *Le Samourai* features long, visually introspective sequences with nearly no dialogue or sound at all.

Le Samourai was one of many films Woo watched as a teenager, during his days with the Chinese Student Weekly Theatre Company. Woo was profoundly impressed by *Le Samourai* and continues to list it as his favorite movie of all time. He says, "*Le Samourai* is the closest thing to a perfect movie I have ever seen. It is an amazingly pure and elegant film about a criminal who is facing death and coming to terms with a life devoted to violence—to inflicting death on others. The picture has been a major influence on my work, not only because of the story and the way it is shot, but also because it is a gangster film that is as much about the way a gangster thinks and feels as about the way that he behaves. Melville understands that Jeff, played by Alain Delon, is doomed to be killed because he is a killer himself, that the way he is bound to die is built into the way he lives. When he chose his life, he was embracing his own death. He achieves redemption at the end by accepting his fate gracefully. To me, this is the most romantic attitude imaginable."

The moment Woo started writing *A Better Tomorrow* (1986) he felt that this was his chance to make his *Le Samourai*, and he was not going to pull any punches while doing it. He couldn't believe he was finally getting this chance, which resulted in an urgency and a determination to make this opportunity count.

Hark would produce the movie for his new company and Woo would direct. Hark saw producing as his next logical step; he would not concentrate all his time and efforts on only one film, he would be involved in several at once.

As the script progressed, it became clear that this project would not proceed smoothly. Hark says, "I got too involved in the project—there was not enough room for the director to breathe. John Woo is very much an independent."

Woo saw that this was his chance to make the kind of movie he had been dreaming about, and he was not about to back down. *A Better Tomorrow* was inspired by a black-and-white Cantonese movie made in 1964 called *True Colors of a Hero.*

Terence Chang, who worked in the production office during the making of *A Better Tomorrow* and who later became a full producing partner of Woo's said, "John's film isn't exactly a remake (of *True Colors of a Hero*) because he added a lot and changed the characters around quite a bit. But the themes are the same."

After *A Better Tomorrow* was written, Woo and Hark started making the rounds for financing.

Karl Maka ran Golden Princess, a Hong Kong movie studio that wasn't afraid to back independent movies. He remembers the day that Woo and Hark came into his office with the pitch for *A Better Tomorrow.* "I never want to hear what their story was. They wanted to tell me all this stuff about brotherhood and friends betraying each other. I stopped them. 'How many stars in the film?' They tell me there are three and one of them is Leslie Cheung, who was a very popular singer at the time. 'How much of the running time will be action sequences?' They told me about one-third of the total running time would be action. I ask them, 'How much will it cost?' They gave me a figure and I said, 'Okay.' That was how movies were made in Hong Kong."

A Better Tomorrow begins with fellow triad members Ho (Ti Lung) and Mark (Chow Yun-Fat) making a counterfeit currency transaction with some foreign criminals in an office tower in downtown Hong Kong. After a celebration of their score, Ho is then sent to Taiwan by his boss on another mission. In Taiwan Ho is betrayed by the crooks he was to do business with. He is sent to a Taiwanese prison. Ho's younger brother Kit (Leslie Cheung) has just graduated from the Hong Kong police academy and is completely shattered when he hears that his brother, whom he idolized, is a criminal, and in prison.

Mark heads to Taiwan to exact revenge for what happened to Ho. He is shot and severely wounded in the process.

A few years later Ho is released from prison to find that his brother is embittered towards him because his criminal status has prevented Kit from rising in the police ranks. Ho pleads with his brother for forgiveness and tells him that he will leave his criminal behavior in the past. Kit is far too angry to accept that and tells his brother that should he commit any further crimes, Kit will gladly arrest him.

Ho is a beaten man and realizes that going straight is his only hope. He takes a job at a taxi company that hires ex-cons to give them a second start.

Mark is now a crippled man who is forced to wash car windows for tips while the man who betrayed Ho is the top man in the triad. Ho sees Mark washing the windshield of the triad boss, the man who betrayed him, for a handful of change.

Ho emotionally reunites with Mark. Ho had no idea Mark was wounded trying to avenge Ho's betrayal.

Mark and Ho join forces to battle the triad and kill the boss who has ruined both of their lives.

The movie ends with a massive gunfight. Mark dies in a barrage of gunfire, sacrificing his life to kill the triad boss. The police arrive, including Kit, and the estranged brothers are brought together.

The direction of *A Better Tomorrow* is cool and stylish, with clever stylization of the gunfights. Woo creates wonderfully tense moments, like the scene in which Mark goes to Taiwan to kill the gangsters that betrayed Ho. Mark walks down a nightclub hallway in slow-motion, a girl on each arm. As he passes a large planter he slips an automatic pistol into the greenery. The scene then cuts to the inside of a lounge where several gangsters sit at a table gambling. The white doors to the lounge slide slowly open, revealing Mark with an automatic pistol in each hand. With cool, methodical precision Mark proceeds to blast everyone in the room, not once, but several times apiece.

He throws his guns aside and exits the lounge. A wounded thug follows him out into the hall. Mark reaches for the conveniently stashed pistol and smoothly fires on the thug. The editing of this sequence is so perfect that even audience members who shy away from scenes of violence must see this scene for the brilliant direction it really is.

Hong Kong-based movie critic Shu Kei refers to that particular scene as "the guilty pleasure" one gets from watching a Woo movie. Quentin Tarantino also waxed enthusiastic, stating, "That was fucking brilliant! You could line up ten of the best American action movies in a row and none of them had anything as clever as that."

The three stars in *A Better Tomorrow* are Ti Lung as Ho, Leslie Cheung as his idealistic younger brother, Kit, and Chow Yun-Fat as the charismatic Mark Gor (who, as a triad enforcer, is referred to as "Brother Mark" throughout the movie).

In 1966 when he was eighteen, Lung was working as an apprentice tailor in Kowloon, but on a whim he decided to audition for the Shaw Brothers Studio. He was accepted and trained in acting, stunts and horsemanship. Lung's debonair good looks and his accelerated progress in all acting endeavors caught the eye of the legendary director Chang Cheh. Cheh put Lung in *Return of the One-Armed Swordsman*, which starred kung-fu superstar Jimmy Wang Yu. From the mid- to late seventies Lung received international acclaim for such movies as *Blood Brothers* (1973), also known as *Dynasty of Blood*, on which Woo had worked as an assistant director, and *Magic Blade and Avenging Eagle* (1979). Lung worked exclusively for Shaw Brothers until 1980 when his popularity suddenly waned. He went off to Taiwan where he made eight movies in rapid succession before Shaw Brothers brought him back in 1981. He worked sporadically until Shaw Brothers stopped making movies altogether, at which time he found himself no longer in demand at all. His career was resuscitated by his friend Woo when he was cast in *A Better Tomorrow*.

Cheung attended school in England before returning to Hong Kong. In 1980, while still in his teens, he entered a singing contest and was offered a role in a drama series on Rediffusion TV. He continued to sing and was also signed to a record deal at Polygram. He had already made eight movies when Woo cast him as Kit in *A Better Tomorrow*, which made him a star. What sets Cheung apart in Hong Kong is that he chooses his roles carefully, which is unusual for Asian actors. Most are under strict contract and act when and for whom they are told.

After reprising his role as Kit in *A Better Tomorrow II* (1987) Cheung made the acclaimed *Days of Being Wild* (1991) for iconoclastic Hong Kong filmmaker Wong Kar-wai. He then became bored and came close to quitting acting altogether. He announced that he had decided to go back to school in Canada, but his plans changed when he was cast as the effeminate opera singer in the Chinese hit *Farewell My Concubine* (1993) from director Chen

Kaige (Cheung also starred in Kaige's *Temptress Moon* in 1996). Cheung, always looking for an adventurous project, tried very hard to convince Canadian director David Cronenberg to cast him in his big-budgeted version of the hit play *M. Butterfly* (1993) only to lose out to *The Last Emperor* (1987) star John Lone.

When asked about working with Woo, Cheung was complimentary. "John is such a professional. He writes a good script then he sticks to it. He has real feelings for each of the characters he writes. That is great for an actor because it inspires confidence. I ran into John at the Oscars and we discussed working together again. I hope that can happen."

A Better Tomorrow particularly showcased the talents of Chow Yun-Fat. Yun-Fat had been around for years and was well known as a dashing young romantic lead in several television soap operas, but he had not before been seen in a role as dark and menacing as in *A Better Tomorrow*. Yun-Fat is a terrific actor who knows when to take a less-is-more approach. There is a moving moment in the film when Ho returns from his Taiwanese prison to look up his old friend Mark. When Mark sees his friend there is a look of joy on his face, which is quickly tempered by feelings of profound loss. Yun-Fat, rather than going the grand route of crying openly, instead chooses to fight back the emotions. It is a memorable acting moment in a movie that is thought of more for its gunplay and violence.

In the same fashion that Toshiro Mifune was the alter ego of director Akira Kurosawa and Alain Delon was the alter ego of Jean-Pierre Melville, Woo feels a close association with his favorite actor, Yun-Fat. "Chow is kind of my hero. He has a very special quality as an actor. His acting is so natural and so true, from his heart. Also, I like his personality, his real character. He likes to help people. He's a real shining knight to me."

Woo went on to confirm his alter ego theory further by saying, "Usually, when Chow Yun-Fat and I work together, we put our real feelings into the characters. When you see Chow Yun-Fat in one of my movies, you see me. I put myself into his characters."

One thing that Woo always points out when talking about his friend and collaborator is his generosity. Yun-Fat is known for helping out other young actors, not only with a good word but also with money and shelter when needed.

A perhaps-unexpected part of the success of *A Better Tomorrow* was the image of Mark Gor. Credit for this look can be divided equally amongst Yun-Fat, Woo and Hark. A long trenchcoat, aviator sunglasses, a matchstick clenched between his teeth—it was a look by which nineties cinema phenomenon Quentin Tarantino was heavily influenced. "After I saw *A Better Tomorrow*, I went out and bought a long coat. I got identical sunglasses, and I walked around for two weeks dressing like Chow Yun-Fat. To me, that is the ultimate compliment to an action hero—when you want to go around dressed like the guy."

The sunglasses Yun-Fat wore in the movie were, by no coincidence, French actor Alain Delon's signature brand, imported from France. After *A Better Tomorrow* was released the sunglasses sold out all over Hong Kong in less than a week—stores couldn't keep them in stock. Alain Delon sent Yun-Fat a letter thanking him for inadvertently plugging the shades and making them wildly successful.

An interesting side note, both Woo and Hark appear in *A Better Tomorrow*. Woo can be seen in a couple of sequences as a strangely benevolent law-enforcement officer, and Hark can be seen in a more comic turn, in the scene at the cello audition.

A Better Tomorrow was a huge critical and commercial hit, becoming the highest-grossing movie in the history of Hong Kong cinema. In fact, many credit it with being the movie that changed Hong Kong action cinema forever. But it was not the first Hong Kong gangster picture to impress international audiences. Director Johnny Mak made a much-lauded film called *The Long Arm of the Law* in 1984, a hard-hitting, pull-no-punches movie that depicted a gang of Chinese mobsters pulling jewel heists in Hong Kong. Mak's movie introduced an element of realism into Chinese thrillers that hadn't existed before. Mak consulted real gangsters, some of whom had committed armed heists, to ensure the authenticity of the story. With *A Better Tomorrow*

Woo set a new standard in quality, bringing surrealism and visual poetry to action sequences that stunned viewers.

A Better Tomorrow was the film that Woo had been waiting many years to make, and he speaks passionately about what he wanted to convey. "It's not a gangster movie specifically. It's a film about chivalry and honor, but set in a modern world. I want a new generation to ask: 'What is friendship? What is brotherhood? What have we lost?' I wanted to play up the violence in *A Better Tomorrow*. I exaggerated blood and death to make the audiences sense the invisible and widespread power of the underworld. The film was also inspired and influenced in part by Zhang Che's martial-arts films. Not so much in the way of portraying violence, but in his unrestrained way of writing about emotions and chivalry. Chinese cinema has always been too low-key. We should be more expressive, put more of ourselves into our films."

Stanley Tong, director of Jackie Chan's *Supercop* (1992), served as stunt double on *A Better Tomorrow*. He thinks he understands the appeal of Woo's movies: "In Chinese culture there are four things, four qualities that everyone must know—*Jung* is loyalty; *Xiao* is being loyal to your parents; *Ren* is being good to people in general, forgiving them when they are trying to harm you; and *Yi*, which means when you are a friend you are willing to give your life for your friend. John Woo's movies contain these elements with which most people identify."

That *A Better Tomorrow* became a huge hit, elevating Woo to a higher level within the industry, was no fluke. The movie is well-made and well-written. The script is often overshadowed by the phenomenal action sequences, but Woo successfully infused the movie with a strong sense of loss, loyalty and feeling—not an easy thing to do when underworld figures are your main protagonists. Woo managed to make characters who were not likable on the surface compelling and worth caring about. *A Better Tomorrow* looks like a cheaply made movie, but Woo made the most of what he had to work with. That grit gives the movie an authentic feel—a fortunate byproduct of the lack of money he had to work with.

Even though *A Better Tomorrow* firmly placed both Woo and Hark on the international cinematic map, their working relationship throughout the making of the movie was a contentious one. Because Hark was such a hands-on producer there were constant discussions about where certain sequences were going. Woo was forced to justify, and then stick to his guns, so to speak, if he was going to make the movie that he wanted to make.

The success of *A Better Tomorrow* provoked a wave of imitations around the world, but particularly in Hong Kong, where it was even copied outright. Some of these quickie rip-off versions of *A Better Tomorrow* came close to matching Woo's level of bloodshed and his body count, but few could touch the style and the passion that went into its making. There was one exception, *City on Fire* (1987), directed by Ringo Lam, another protégé of Cinema City. A long-time friend of Lam's, Yun-Fat starred in the movie, with the result that *City on Fire*, on the heels of *A Better Tomorrow*, helped to solidify realism and boldness as signatures in Hong Kong action movies.

Woo is known for his reluctance to repeat what he's already done. So, perhaps it was in response to the imitators that he signed on to do a sequel, *A Better Tomorrow II* (1987). In this film, the story focuses on Kit, the young policeman. Now that Mark Gor is dead and Kit's brother Ho is back behind bars, Kit is determined to start making up for lost time in his career. When Ho refuses to accept probation in exchange for assisting the authorities in their investigation of his former mentor, the shipping magnate Lung (played by Dean Shek), Kit turns his back on his home life and his pregnant wife in order to go undercover to get close to Lung's daughter, and then ultimately to Lung.

Lung is now reformed but is being pressured by counterfeiters who want to use his shipyards for their illegal activities. When Ho finds out that his younger brother is involved in the undercover investigation he quickly agrees to the early-release offer so he can get back to the streets to protect his volatile young brother. Lung soon finds himself framed for a gangland assassination. He quickly heads to New York, leaving his daughter Peggy in Kit's care. Peggy is promptly murdered.

While Ho remains in Hong Kong, Lung is slowly slipping into madness in New York. He descends to the point where he ends up in a padded cell. It is here that Yun-Fat makes his return as Ken, Mark Gor's twin brother, who is working as a New York City restaurateur. Ken comes to the aid of Lung and manages to save him from complete insanity.

Meanwhile, back in Hong Kong, Ho has volunteered to go undercover to join forces with Lung's betrayer, a crook named Ko, so he can settle matters himself. But as Ho gets closer to his subject, Ko then insists that Ho shoot Kit as a test of his loyalty and courage.

One reason Woo consented to make *A Better Tomorrow II* was concern for his friends. "Dean Shek (once a popular Hong Kong comedian) was having a lot of money problems at the time and, since we were all friends, we agreed to make *A Better Tomorrow II*, giving him a big part, to help him out."

Shek was known for his broadly comedic roles, often in Jackie Chan movies like *Snake in the Eagle's Shadow* and *Drunken Master* (both released in 1978), but Woo cast him in a very dramatic, complex role as a tortured mob boss who is brought back from the brink of complete insanity by Mark Gor's twin brother.

A Better Tomorrow II isn't a simple continuation of the story begun in *A Better Tomorrow*, but rather a fun-house exaggeration of the central motifs explored in the original. All of Woo's trademarks are evident—slow-motion action sequences, high-caliber chivalry and entertaining excessiveness.

Because it is a sequel, *A Better Tomorrow II* lacks the original magic of its predecessor, but there are moments of brilliance in the final section of the movie. The gunfight that ends *A Better Tomorrow II* must be seen to be believed. Everything from samurai swords to hand grenades are brought into play.

In one spectacular stunt involving a large explosion, Yun-Fat was almost killed for real. He was a bit closer to the flames than he should have been and was knocked over and stunned by the blast.

The gunfight so impressed Quentin Tarantino that he wrote it into his screenplay for *True Romance* (1993). Watch Tony Scott's *True Romance* and pay special attention to the scene where Clarence (Christian Slater) heads out of his apartment to kill Drexl (Gary Oldman), a villain in the movie. His girlfriend Alabama (Patricia Arquette) stays behind in the apartment watching a movie on television. The movie is *A Better Tomorrow II* and the sequence we see is the climactic gunfight.

A Better Tomorrow II was a huge success for the same reason that many sequels are successful—it cashed in on a popular title. Critically, the movie met with mixed reaction. Critic Ric Meyer wrote in his review of *A Better Tomorrow II*, "A funhouse reflection on the original that manages to be both a satire and an homage. As such, it is at times almost more exhilarating, because we no longer have any real emotional investment in the characters' plagiarized personalities. We are free to be thrilled without worry, as dozens upon dozens of white-suited gunsels are mown down— falling out of closets in contorting waves like clowns tumbling out of a circus Volkswagen." One San Francisco-based critic colorfully wrote, "Painting the world exit-wound red, this film confirms that in Hell, there are no dry-cleaners."

Like the original, *A Better Tomorrow II* was fraught with problems because of the constant friction between John Woo and Tsui Hark. They fought about the script and then fought about the editing. Upon completion of filming *A Better Tomorrow II* Woo delivered a print of his version to the studio. It ran close to two hours and forty minutes in length—a lot longer than the studio wanted it to be. In fact, the studio was furious and demanded that Woo cut the film down to a more-releasable two hours or less—and furthermore, to edit it within a week. Woo remembers, "Tsui Hark took one half of the film and I took the other half— we cut our halves down separately so I never really saw the entire movie until opening night. Needless to say, I found the whole thing uneven and unsatisfying."

Woo has, by and large, disassociated himself from the movie with the exception of the final shoot-out, which he refers to as his "mad painting." Critic and Vancouver Film Festival programmer Tony Rayns wrote, "John Woo himself asked me not to see this film, and he said that it was 'the worst film ever made.' He was wrong of course, but you can clearly see that this film was made under duress."

After the wild success of these two movies, both Woo and Hark were so flushed with their own notoriety that they decided to keep the momentum going. Woo proposed the idea of making a prequel to the *A Better Tomorrow* movies. He suggested that the movie be set in sixties war-torn Vietnam, and was already hard at work on the screenplay when Hark announced to the media that he, and not Woo, would be directing the third installment of the series. This was the first that Woo had heard about being removed from the project and it bothered him profoundly.

Hark went ahead and foolhardily produced and directed the third installment himself, calling it *A Better Tomorrow III* (1989). The finished product is a wide departure from the first two movies and was received with just as wide a difference of opinion. *A Better Tomorrow III* takes place in 1974, well before the stories in the first two movies. Mark Gor (again well-played by Yun-Fat) is taught to fire weapons and is given his trademark trenchcoat and sunglasses by an old girlfriend, played by popular singer Anita Mui.

The story is a long-winded saga, with a lot less reliance on action. However, *A Better Tomorrow III* is visually compelling and stylized to maximum effect.

A difference in the styles of Woo and Hark can be seen in sequences involving tension-filled stand-offs. The stand-off scene at the end of *A Better Tomorrow III* lacks the cool ironic humor that Woo casually injects in his stand-off sequences. Hark shows that he knows where to put a camera to make things visually interesting, but his writing, editing and sense of pacing are not up to the standard set by Woo (for more evidence of this, see Hark's 1998 American film *Knock-off* starring Hong Kong action-director favorite Jean-Claude Van Damme).

Yun-Fat, now an action-movie superstar thanks to the first two *A Better Tomorrow* movies, was happy to have a serious role that he was familiar with but could still take to even greater depths than he had before. But he was anxious about the way the story was set up. "I was worried that the audience wouldn't believe Mark Gor had learned everything he knew from a beautiful young woman."

Film Comment writer Howard Hampton stated that *A Better Tomorrow III* was, "a project stolen both figuratively and literally from John Woo," but Hark doesn't believe that to be the case. Hark, who was raised in Saigon, says, "I wanted to go back there to see what happened. Friends and relatives had been telling me some really shocking stories about the war."

The success of the first two *A Better Tomorrow* movies almost overwhelmed Woo. This was the level of achievement he had actively pursued for so many years. Yet instead of feeling vindicated by making these movies his way, Woo felt uneasy. "After the big hits that *A Better Tomorrow* parts *I* and *II* were, I was confused. I was wondering, 'Who am I and what kind of movies do I want to make?' I was suddenly established as an action director, but I felt the immediate need to change people's impressions of me. I knew that my movies were not only about action, I knew that I poured a lot of ideas into them, but people didn't seem to notice that and it was bothering me."

After *A Better Tomorrow* Woo's action-driven war movie *Heroes Shed No Tears* was released. It was actually made five years earlier yet remained on the shelf until 1986. Golden Harvest decided to cash in on Woo's suddenly very-hot name by getting another of his films into theaters as quickly as possible. But Golden Harvest severely edited the movie to cut its running time, thus enabling it to be shown more times per day, increasing its chances at profitability.

Heroes Shed No Tears is nowhere near as slick as his later movies, but it does have a dark, visual harshness that indicates Woo knew the direction in which he wanted to travel. It also contains a number of classic Woo moments. There is a terrific moment of tenderness when a young boy softly touches the battle scars on his father's back.

Another sequence shows a corrupt general setting a cane field on fire, trapping the hero's little boy in the middle of the flames. Woo cuts between shots of the terrified boy dodging the flames, trying to find a way out, scenes of the general watching. Just when you think the general's humanity will kick in and that he'll rescue the boy, he smiles sinisterly, climbs aboard his jeep and drives off. Ingeniously, the little boy buries himself under a layer of dirt until the fire burns itself out. The movie proves that Woo has a terrific instinct for when to insert poignancy amidst the gunfire, explosions and fiery scenes.

The very fact that *Heroes Shed No Tears* was brought back to life, based solely on John Woo's name, after five years of dormancy proved that he was now in a position of power—the kind of power he had never dreamed of. Now he had to decide how to use it.

Five

1989-1992:
WOO ASSERTS HIMSELF

A misprint on a prop road sign in **The Killer:**
Instead of reading "Sacred Heart Hospital" it read
"Scared Heart Hospital."

A Better Tomorrow may have changed Hong Kong cinema forever and may have put Woo on the cinematic map internationally, but it was only a hint of what was to come. Woo was now in a position to proceed in a direction of his own choosing and to do so knowing that international film audiences were supportive.

In 1989 Woo made a curious movie called *Just Heroes.* It has all the ingredients of being another terrific Woo "heroic bloodshed" gangster movie, but it doesn't quite come together. This violent crime drama is about a Hong Kong triad boss named Tsou who is betrayed and killed. Each of his three adopted sons are possible heirs to his criminal empire, and one of them is the traitor and killer. Woo adeptly keeps his audience guessing as to which of the three sons is the killer. It stars Danny Lee, who Woo would later use to greater effect in *The Killer* (1989), but the characters in this movie don't possess the same strength or moral certainty as the characters in the *A Better Tomorrow* films. It does, however, contain many of the Woo trademarks—the cool posturing of tough guys who talk a lot about loyalty while blasting away at one another with every make and model of firearm available.

Just Heroes was produced by Hark and must be considered a blip on the otherwise wildly successful career partnership of Hark and Woo. They would next make the icy-cool film noir *The Killer* and set the cinematic world on its ear.

Woo, who has frequently declared his love for the work of Jean-Pierre Melville, particularly his classic noir film *Le Samourai*, finally got the chance to pour all that inspiration into this magnificent movie that pays considerable homage to the Melville classic. Melville aside, there was another cinematic influence that Woo mentions: "I was also fascinated by a Japanese movie from the sixties. I forgot the name of the movie but it starred Takakura Ken, and was shot in Hong Kong and Macau. Takakura Ken was a killer who had principles; he would only kill bad people. But he goes to Hong Kong to do a job, and he discovers that he has been used by the gang to kill a good person. So the killer tries to find out who set him up and take revenge on the whole gang. And somehow a Japanese woman, a prostitute, who had TB and wanted to get back to Japan, catches his fancy. He promises her that after he takes his revenge he will take her back to Japan, and see to it that she gets the proper treatment. So off he goes to fight the gang, and he gets killed. And there is a scene that takes place the next morning, the girl is still waiting on the dock, but the hero never comes to take her home. I loved this movie very much and tried to get some of the spirit of it into *The Killer*." But it was Melville and *Le Samourai* that Woo was most interested in—its influence here is so prevalent that some sequences are almost exact copies.

The Killer was financed by Golden Princess, who happened to have Yun-Fat under a personal services contract. Hark's Film Workshop would act as the official production company. This film would mark the last professional association of Woo and Hark, and the end of their friendship. Once *The Killer* became an international hit, Tri-Star Pictures in Hollywood purchased the rights to remake it—but Hark refused to share the buyout money or the credit, stating, "I'm sorry but the storyline for *The Killer* was written entirely by me."

Terence Chang, now Woo's partner and producer of many of his later films, was Hark's general manager at Film Workshop during the making of *The Killer*. "Let me set the record straight," states Chang. "After *A Better Tomorrow II* Tsui Hark said that John Woo had screwed up the movie. He even asked me to fire John. I refused. So after that, Tsui Hark would reject every idea proposed by John, including *The Killer* and the project that developed into *Once A Thief* (1990), until John was flat broke. Can you imagine it? Here was a top director reduced to borrowing money from Chow Yun-Fat."

Yun-Fat confirms this view of events. He went to the bosses at Golden Princess and told them that he was very interested in making *The Killer*. When they talked to Hark about the project, he told them to pass. He completely disowned the project saying it was unworthy and no different than all the other run-of-the-mill gangster movies that were inspired by the *A Better Tomorrow* movies. Yun-Fat insisted that Golden Princess make *The Killer* and that it be the next movie that he did for them.

When asked why he and Woo are no longer friends, Hark gives a curious answer. "I don't understand what happened. Suddenly we just stopped talking to each other. A lot of people around him just started getting hostile. I remember one time, John was given an award of some kind for *The Killer*, and nobody even bothered to tell me about the win. That was the beginning of my feelings that there was something seriously wrong between John Woo and I."

Woo's nature does not allow him to discuss the situation with any vitriol, but his disappointment is clear. "I remember getting offers, some of them for a lot of money, to leave Film Workshop and Tsui Hark, but I chose to remain and stay loyal to Tsui Hark because he gave me a second chance. I wouldn't even let anyone say a bad thing about him. If anyone did, I would get very angry and want to beat the guy up." After the release of *The Killer* Woo and Chang decided to form their own production company called Milestone Pictures (with Linda Kuk). Woo remains generous to the end though. "Tsui Hark and I just have different ideas," says Woo. "I still think he is a great talent."

The Killer is a fascinatingly layered story about a hitman named Jeff (Yun-Fat) who decides to quit the life of crime that he has been leading after doing one last job for someone he considers a friend. During that hit he accidentally blinds a nightclub singer. Jeff is a man with a conscience despite his chosen profession. He keeps tabs on the wounded Jenny, even helping her out when she is being mugged, and insinuating himself into her life as a potential suitor.

During this budding romance a highly principled Hong Kong detective (played with perfect, tightly coiled energy by Danny Lee) chases a criminal onto a crowded city bus. The criminal takes a hostage, but the detective fires on him anyway. The criminal is killed, but so is another passenger on the bus who dies of a heart attack during the violence. The detective is reprimanded, and ends up on the case of trying to find out who killed the gangsters and injured the singer in the nightclub.

Jeff decides to take one more job, a lucrative hit on a top crooked Hong Kong businessman during the opening of a dragon boat race, to earn enough money to take Jenny to America for an operation that will restore her sight. Jeff doesn't know that he is being set up. A retired hitman is dangerous to those who have hired him in the past, so he cannot be allowed to retire and walk off happily into the sunset.

The detective learns that there might be an attempt on the life of the businessman and is on hand. Jeff assassinates the businessman from a clever vantage point of a speedboat in the harbor. Once the kill is made Jeff takes off in the boat. Then the detective jumps into a boat and gives chase. Jeff makes it to the island rendezvous point only to have his people open fire on him. The detective arrives on the beach just in time to get into the fray. Again an innocent is hit in the crossfire. This time it is a little girl who smiles at Jeff when he comes onto the beach. Jeff does away with the bad guys and urgently bundles up the wounded girl to take her to the nearest hospital. The detective witnesses this and gains some respect for this killer.

Upon further investigation the detective realizes that the assassin that he pursued in the boat, the man who is seeing Jenny, is the man responsible for blinding her.

As the detective closes in on Jeff he realizes that they aren't all that dissimilar. Both Jeff and the detective battle the assassins in a church in a spectacular, highly symbolic gunfight that leaves them both mortally wounded.

The Killer is an exceedingly well-made action movie from every angle. The writing is economical and highly effective. The acting, especially that of Yun-Fat and Lee, is first rate, and the direction of the action sequences is an action-film fan's dream come true. This movie proves that Woo is a filmmaker with style to burn. At the same time, the film has so many metaphors as well as religious iconography that it also provides film scholars with more than enough to ponder over. Given Woo's religious background, it is rather remarkable to watch a statue of the Virgin Mary explode in the church during the climactic gunfight.

Woo is quick to explain: "To me, she (the Virgin Mary) symbolizes all that is good and pure. When the villains destroy the statue, it is like they are destroying the last goodness."

Chang was fascinated by the whole project, and Woo's relationship to the material. "I think John is a very interesting person because he is so full of contradictions. I mean, Jeff (the Chow Yun-Fat character) kills people for money. But to John he also represents justice."

Woo elaborates on this theme. "The killer is a man who does bad things, but he wants to be good. That's why I put him in a church at the movie's beginning. He is fed up with killing and he wants to stop. He goes to the church like I did in my childhood. I always liked to sit in the church because I liked the peace. I used to sit there and think about God, think about fate, ask who was controlling my destiny, God or myself."

From the opening sequence, an ultra-cool shootout in the back room of a nightclub, through to the grand-finale bullet barrage in the church, and in every action sequence in between, the violent confrontations are staged with a modern-dance-like choreography that makes *The Killer* fun to watch more than once.

There are other moments in *The Killer* that have since been aped by many "cool" young filmmakers. In one scene, a little girl is wounded in the crossfire. Jeff takes her to the hospital while the police are in hot pursuit. In the hospital the two adversaries, Jeff and his policeman nemesis, stand with guns aimed at each other's heads while Jeff coolly utters, "Don't bother the doctor." That image of foes standing with guns jammed in each other's temples is common in Woo's movies. The notion of mutually assured destruction is now a common staple in crime films these days, but no one does it as well as Woo. It is not the image of the confrontation itself that is so dramatic, but rather knowing just how long to sustain it, and what the characters should say to one another during the standoff that can make it so compelling. No filmmaker can match Woo when it comes to these sorts of sensitivities.

Ric Meyers, a regular columnist for *Inside Kung-Fu* magazine and the author of *The Encyclopedia of Martial Arts Movies*, gave a lengthy rave of the movie. "An amoral cop hunts a moral assassin, allowing John Woo to choreograph a dance of death that reaches its height as the two characters tango around each other, their guns in each others' faces, while the woman the hitman accidentally blinded obliviously makes tea for them. It is one of the greatest black comic moments in movie history."

Interestingly, this movie was meant to be an epic-length, action-filled ponderance on the nature of criminal activity and the thought patterns of cops and criminals as they go about their dangerous business. Woo's first cut of the movie was a lengthy 142 minutes, thirty-two minutes longer than the version commonly available. Woo himself made the decision to cut his masterpiece following the film's initial release in Hong Kong. The exised material was a sub-plot involving an emotionally complex relationship between Jeff and his best friend, another hitman working within the same triad. That relationship, bolstered by the solid performance of Chu Kong, remains in the movie, but only in a cursory way as a device to keep the action moving with a logical motivation. Woo liked the sub-plot and thought it was important to the film, but he felt he had to be true to his characters.

"Sidney [Chu Kong] is a tragic figure," says Woo. "He is Jeff's best friend, but, as Jeff understands, Sidney lives by a gangster's code that rigidly dictates behavior. A hitman who is spotted on the job is rubbed out—and his go-between has to be the one who pulls the trigger." This underworld code was echoed a decade later in the brilliant Mike Newell American mob movie *Donnie Brasco* (1997) in which Al Pacino explains this philosophy to Johnny Depp.

Part of the cut material was restored for a dubious version of *The Killer* that was available only in Taiwan. In August 1998 this version, described as the only print of the longer version, was screened in Toronto as part of the *Fant-Asia* film festival. On hand at the screening was the editor of the film, David Wu, who was in Toronto working as editor and sometime director of the TV series *John Woo's Once A Thief*. Wu took the stage to answer some questions but said he was really there to see the movie because the re-cut version was done without his knowledge or input. When asked specifically about what was restored Wu said, "I had no idea this version even existed, and if I find out who re-cut this movie without our knowing about it I'm going to kick his butt." The audience laughed as Wu demonstrated just how he was going to kick the phantom editor's butt with a series of martial-arts kicks. It was obvious as the movie unspooled that the restored footage, scenes of Chu Kong and a few scenes of gunfire, was cut in hastily and without much care or skill.

Much has been made of the similarities between Quentin Tarantino's *Reservoir Dogs* (1992) and Ringo Lam's Hong Kong action epic *City on Fire* (1987—which also stars Tarantino-favorite Yun-Fat, and Danny Lee). Tarantino himself is quite open about the inspiration that Hong Kong movies, Woo's in particular, have provided him. His characters in *Reservoir Dogs*, and to a lesser extent in *Pulp Fiction*, act and dress very similarly to the characters in Woo's *A Better Tomorrow* films. As further evidence, the first draft of Tarantino's *Reservoir Dogs* screenplay includes an acknowledgment page (a rarity in film screenplays because the only people who will read it are agents, film executives and actors), which lists Yun-Fat as one of the people he wants to thank for inspiring him.

Woo may be influential, but he is also influenced. Watching *The Killer*, one can see many of the cool elements borrowed from Jean-Pierre Melville's *Le Samourai*. The two-fisted gunfire that is now a trademark of Woo and Yun-Fat is seen in *Le Samourai*. Yun-Fat must have studied the performance of Alain Delon in *Le Samourai*, because he affects many of the same mannerisms. Woo has chosen to dress Yun-Fat much like Delon was dressed in Woo's favorite movie, right down to the white gloves. One of the early scenes in *The Killer* has Yun-Fat's Jeff entering a nightclub and making eye contact with a female singer before going into the back room to conduct some mayhem—a direct copy of a scene in Melville's film.

After the release of *The Killer*, word really started to spread on Woo. Suddenly, Western eyes were on him. Western critics were studying his work in their ridiculously pretentious way, over-analyzing.

Consider how the cinema press treats the exceptionally talented Coen brothers. The Coen brothers, when asked about the allegorical significance of the opening sequence of their film *Miller's Crossing* (1990), which features a fedora being blown down a tree-lined laneway, responded simply—that they made the whole movie because they wanted to make a picture with guys in fedoras carrying machine guns. Woo's approach to filmmaking is equally pragmatic. "Whatever I do, I never think about the audience. The first thing I think of is the character, the actor and I, how we feel. To me, the gangster films are just like the Chinese swordplay films. To me Chow Yun-Fat holding a gun is just like Wang Yu holding a sword. All I intend to glorify is the hero. I do not intend to glorify violence or the triad societies, just the behavior of the hero." However, the success of *The Killer* did force Woo to rethink his philosophy. Some reactions to the film took him by surprise. In Britain *The Killer* was looked upon as far too violent to be shown to anyone but adults, and it was given an X-rating by the ratings board. American ad campaigns for the movie also warned of "extreme graphic violence." "I was really surprised by the reaction that some people had to the movie," remembers Woo. "They were so serious about it! It made me realize I have to be more concerned about how people will react. I think I care too much about romanticism. In the future, [I] have to look deeper into the people. *Bullet in the Head* (1990) [which came after *The Killer*] was my experiment to do that, which is why the movie was made without a hero."

Producer Chang recalls that the attention paid to *The Killer* had a disturbing, reverberating effect. "The success of *The Killer* overseas made a lot of filmmakers and even film critics in Hong Kong jealous. It created a certain kind of resentment in the film industry in Hong Kong. One thing I can say for sure, the American, European, Japanese, Korean and even the Taiwanese audiences and critics appreciated *The Killer* a lot more than the people in Hong Kong. After the rights for an American remake were sold, John and I went off to America to make movies; it got even worse then. That's very unhealthy." This petty resentment might explain why Woo has never looked back to the Hong Kong film industry since his move to Los Angeles.

Actor Yun-Fat has a theory as to why the movie didn't reach a huge audience upon its initial release. "It's the violence," he says. "A lot of people can't stand it, they can't take it. I, myself, don't like violence at all. I don't like gunfire. John Woo does. He loves the sound of bullets firing. On the set, he never bothers to wear ear plugs because he loves the sounds that different guns make."

Adding to the negative publicity surrounding the release of *The Killer* was a reintroduction of an argument between the Hong Kong governmental authorities and Hong Kong filmmakers. Authorities were worried that these violent movies were glorious recruitment campaigns for the Hong Kong triads. They argued that the gangsters were portrayed in a much more romantic and appealing way than the police, and that the films often depicted a code of honor among the criminal fraternity that doesn't actually exist in real life. Yun-Fat was quick to protest this. "You simply cannot blame films for the breakdown of society. It is down to the parents and the education system to teach the new generation. Not the movies."

Easy to say, but in Hong Kong the statistics seem to indicate that Hong Kong action films *are* partly responsible for the breakdown of Hong Kong society. Through the eighties there was a significant rise in the number of people joining the ranks of the Hong Kong triads—something that could reasonably be attributed to the glorification of criminal activity by a wave of popular movies. To be fair, Woo is not entirely to blame for this. Several other directors and actors, particularly actor Andy Lau who seemed to star in a new movie every month during the eighties in which he played a well-dressed, slick-talking gangster, were all part of the wave. But this trend was to take a truly bizarre turn when these real-life mob organizations, the triads, started forming their own production companies for the purposes of making some fast money, and then laundering their profits from other, less reputable sources.

Lau, who starred in movies with such titles as *Bloody Brotherhood* (1987), *God of the Gamblers* (1989), *Gangland Odyssey* (1991) and *Hong Kong Godfather* (1996), found himself being pressured by these triad-owned movie companies to star in their productions. Lau often did make such appearances, though mostly in cameos. Things really got out of hand when Jim Choi, the manager of kung-fu movie superstar Jet Li, was gunned down outside his office for presumably resisting the overtures of triad movie producers.

A rally was organized by several concerned performers, including Yun-Fat and Jackie Chan. The group called themselves Artists Against Violence—a rather ineffective move that didn't speak to the real problem of gangster infiltration of the film industry. Many performers and producers accepted and tolerated the involvement of the triads, which actually boosted film production and gave work to many people that might otherwise be unemployed, provided that no harm came to them and their associates.

The big-budget Universal Pictures movie biography of Bruce Lee (*Dragon: The Bruce Lee Story* in 1993) was partially shot in Hong Kong, and the production had to contend with constant triad harassment. Actor Jason Scott Lee, who played Lee in the film, remembers, "I understand that there was some kind of meeting with some of these guys in which a settlement was reached. I don't know exactly what it was because I think they were trying to protect me from that, but from then on things seemed to run quite smoothly."

This triad interference greatly bothered Woo, and was an influence in his last Hong Kong-filmed movie, *Hard Boiled* (1992). "In my film *Hard Boiled*, both lead characters are cops, so I am hoping that this will encourage kids to become policemen because they see that policemen can be cool guys too."

Because of all the publicity Woo's movies were generating, the Hollywood studios were starting to sit up and take notice. An executive at Universal Pictures, the studio that would ultimately give Woo his first Hollywood movie opportunity, remarked after seeing *The Killer*, "Well, the guy can sure direct an action scene." When this comment reached the ears of Quentin Tarantino he quipped, "Yeah, and Michelangelo can sure paint a ceiling."

Part of the critical response to *The Killer* from the Western world was a predictable allusion to the homoerotic nature of the movie. It was said that Danny Lee's character developed an obsessive love for Yun-Fat's character as circumstances drew them closer. Yun-Fat's character is deeply emotional when he discovers that Chu Kong's character has betrayed him. Woo listens to these critical comments but cannot readily accept them. "People will bring their own preconceptions to a movie," Woo points out. "If they see something in *The Killer* that they consider to be homoerotic, then that's their privilege. For them, it clearly must be there. It's certainly not intentional, but, then, a lot of things people have pointed out about my work were never intended when I made the film."

Surprisingly, when all was said and done, *The Killer* did not do all that well at the Hong Kong box office, but that scarcely mattered in the long run. *Reservoir Dogs* was one of the most talked-about movies at its release, launching Quentin Tarantino's career, but it also didn't do all that well at the box office.

Movies like *The Killer* are referred to as masterpieces, not for one single reason, but for several combined elements that all click into place. (Legendary filmmaker John Ford once said, "Classic films happen purely by accident.") One of *The Killer*'s greatest strengths was the casting; not only of Yun-Fat, who gave a brilliant performance, but also of Danny Lee who, as the intense detective, gives what is easily described as the best performance of his career.

Lee, born Danny Lee Sai Yin, is a fine actor. He is best known for shadowing Yun-Fat in both *The Killer* and in

Ringo Lam's *City on Fire*. Earlier in his career, Lee played a wide variety of parts, but his lack of martial-arts skills kept him out of the larger roles in action movies. He then won critical acclaim for his character work. His performance in *Law With Two Phases* (1984) would win him the Best Actor prize at the Hong Kong Film Awards. Despite this, Lee quickly accepted the fact that he was typecast as the second lead, and quite readily played this niche for all it was worth. Lee eventually decided to form his own production company with the intention of developing lead roles for himself, while continuing to work as a gun for hire for established producers. He called his company Magnum Productions, as he was being compared to Clint Eastwood for his silent, stoic performances.

The making of *The Killer* was not without its hardships. Producer Hark and Woo were at complete odds and often fought bitterly over aspects of the movie. Because it was being officially produced by Film Workshop, Hark was in a position to demand that the autonomy with which Woo had operated in the past be lessened considerably. The first thing to be called into question was Woo's original opening. Woo describes it: "The original opening was in a jazz bar. The killer and the singer are there. She's blind and they are already in love. The singer was performing a jazz song and the killer was playing a saxophone. There were lots of flashbacks to show how he wounded the girl and fell in love with her." Hark objected strenuously to this opening, especially the jazz aspect, because he felt that Hong Kong audiences didn't understand or like jazz all that much, so the bulk of the viewers would be distanced from the movie right off the bat. So Woo altered his opening. "I had to change it to a Chinese song, the kind of song they always use in Hong Kong movies. But still, it's a good song and has good, appropriate lyrics, about how we are all wandering and chasing after love." (Woo would later get his jazz scene. The opening sequence of his last Hong Kong-based movie, *Hard Boiled*, contained an opening sequence in a jazz bar with Yun-Fat playing the saxophone.)

In 1992, the prolific writer-director Walter Hill (*The Driver* [1978], *48 Hours* [1982]) turned in a screenplay titled *The Killer, Based on the Hong Kong Action Film by John Woo* (dated April 6, 1992). The script languished for a year until writers Jim Cash and Jack Epps Jr. (who scripted *Legal Eagles* [1986]) were hired by producers Charles Roven and Robert Cavallo to draft a screenplay based on *The Killer* for Tri-Star Pictures. The original studio press release stated that the screenplay was developed for actors Richard Gere and Denzel Washington. As the reworking of *The Killer* progressed some rather major differences started to surface. In one case, producer/manager Chang pitched another of his clients, Michelle Yeoh, for the movie. Yeoh is a huge star in Asia (she appeared with Jackie Chan in *Supercop*), and was selected to play the female lead opposite Pierce Brosnan's James Bond in MGM's *Tomorrow Never*

Dies (1997). It was quite a coup for Yeoh because she was not cast as a traditional "Bond girl," but James Bond's side-kick, who could fight a lot better than he could. Just before securing *Tomorrow Never Dies* Yeoh was offered the American remake of *The Killer*. Chang remembers, "the producers at Tri-Star were having a bit of a hard time with the story of *The Killer*, with the relationship between the two lead characters. They were afraid that they wouldn't translate properly for an American audience, they were afraid that American audiences would interpret the relationship in homoerotic terms. So they suggested changing the role of the cop to a woman and have Michelle step in." Yeoh was certainly interested, but was more interested in projects that were going into production rather than projects that were in the early stages of development.

By August 23, 1993, the screenplay was in its third draft. The proposed opening sequence was a step-by-step recreation of the Woo original except that the lead character is named Jeff Chambers and is a Caucasian hitman in Hong Kong. The gunfight in the nightclub is recreated almost shot for shot, including Woo's inventive staging of the moment when Jeff (Yun-Fat) runs out of guns and ammo and kicks over a table, sending a gun into the air, which he catches and fires in one fluid motion. The script then makes intriguing, sometimes bizarre, departures from the original. In the Woo movie Jeff returns to the church where we were first introduced to him to have the bullets removed from his back. In the remake screenplay, Jeff Chambers is taken to a Hong Kong slum where, strangely, old women writhe about on the ground after being paid to absorb Jeff's pain.

Another departure is the accelerated, superficial nature of the love story between Chambers and the woman he inadvertently blinded. Woo's film has Jeff, wracked with guilt, falling in love with Jenny, but keeping a noble distance. In the Hollywood version, Jeff and Jenny are naked in her bedroom after their first outing together. The subplot involving Jeff and Jenny replaces most of the psychological parrying between Jeff and the Hong Kong cop, who has been replaced in the Hollywood script by an African-American San Francisco detective.

At the end of Woo's masterpiece, the characters played by Yun-Fat and Lee join forces in a kind of unholy alliance to do battle with the greater evil of the triad gangsters trying to kill them. The shootout is deliriously frenetic and takes place in the highly symbolic location of the church that was the setting for the opening shots. The Hollywood script has this final gunfight in an ancient monastery, with monks joining in with their bows and arrows and swords.

The Hollywood remake of *The Killer* will probably never happen. The original is a masterpiece and the risk of unfavorable comparison is simply too high, as the original is widely available on videocassette. However, the rights to remake the movie are still current and every now and then the project is tabled for discussion. Yet the very dynamics of *The Killer*'s story line do not lend themselves to the Hollywood way of making films. In Hollywood-produced studio films, there is an apparent need for everything to turn out right by the end of the film, for the bad guy to get whatever he deserves. In *The Killer*, we have a cop who breaks the law to achieve the results he believes to be "right," and a hired killer who shows himself to have compassion and a conscience whenever he is faced with a true moral dilemma.

Tri-Star Pictures wanted very much for Woo to remake his movie, but Woo would have none of it, stating, "Remake my own movie? Why would I even consider such a thing? What could I possibly add to it?" Ironically, some time later, Woo did a direct remake of one of his own movies, *John Woo's Once A Thief*, for television.

With the success of *The Killer* under his belt, rather than bolting for Hollywood prematurely, Woo had the foresight to consolidate the power and momentum that was swirling around him in Hong Kong. He had a few epics in him, and one would be his next movie. His next movie, released in 1990, would be a Vietnam war epic with the audacious title *Bullet in the Head*. Some consider it his finest work, others simply describe it as another example of the steadily climbing trajectory of his work.

When Woo's career is discussed, focus is usually on the big two, *The Killer* and *Hard Boiled,* as evidence of his style and skill. *Bullet in the Head* deserves the same high regard. It has been written that *Bullet in the Head* is Woo's *Deer Hunter* or his equivalent to *The Good, The Bad, and the Ugly,* and these comparisons are legitimate. The movie is both a departure for Woo and a consolidation of his talents. It is heavier, deeper and perhaps the most personal statement that Woo has ever put on film.

Bullet in the Head is the story of three boys in the slums of Hong Kong in the sixties who grow up as good friends, but become enemies. Ben (Tony Leung) is a romantic and righteous person. Paul (Waise Lee) has an inferiority complex and is determined to become rich, as quickly as he can, and at any cost. Frank (Jackie Cheung) is a happy-go-lucky kind of guy who seems to make the best of whatever situation he is in. He regards his two friends as his heroes.

Ben wants to marry his girlfriend Jane (Fennie Yuen), so Frank borrows money from a local loan shark to pay for the wedding banquet. He ends up being robbed and beaten by a thug named Ringo. Ben is touched by Frank's gesture and enraged by the mugging. In a bloody and very violent confrontation, Ben kills Ringo on the night that he and Jane were to be married. In a panic, Ben and his two friends flee Hong Kong and head to Saigon.

This was Vietnam in 1967. Even though the war was raging throughout the outlying areas of the country, Saigon appeared to be prosperous and peaceful. Ben, Paul and Frank arrive with as much contraband as they can carry so that they might sell it to black marketers for enough money to start new lives. They are dealt another harsh blow when their contraband is destroyed during a riot.

They befriend a Eurasian hitman named Luke (Simon Yam) who works for a local mob leader named Leung (Chung Lam). Luke is in love with a woman named Sally (Yolinda Yan) who is a small-time lounge singer, and a prostitute for Leung. She too is from Hong Kong.

Luke devises a plan to steal gold from Leung so that he and Sally can escape from the boss's iron-handed rule. But Luke cannot pull off this robbery himself. He enlists the help of Ben, Paul and Frank. They steal the gold, which turns out not to belong to Leung, but to a corrupt official in the South Vietnamese army. Enraged, he sends a unit of his soldiers to kill the robbers and retrieve the gold. The soldiers find them hiding in a village, and a vicious gun battle ensues, in which Sally is killed.

Ben, Paul and Frank manage to get away, but the Viet Cong mistake them for South Vietnamese spies, and take them prisoner. They are put in a POW camp where they are tortured, and the worst aspects of their natures are revealed. American forces eventually free them, but by this point Paul is completely consumed by greed. Determined to have the gold at any cost, he puts a bullet in Frank's head and takes the gold. Frank does not die of his wounds, but the bullet remains lodged in his head, requiring constant morphine to control the pain. He has also completely lost his memory. Ben is devastated by Frank's deterioration and ends Frank's suffering by killing him.

In 1974, Ben returns to Hong Kong as a Vietnamese refugee. Paul has become a top Hong Kong gangster with all the money and nefarious prestige he always desired. It's Ben's plan to confront Paul and present him with Frank's skull.

Bullet in the Head is a movie of grand proportion, with big action sequences and big vistas, but at its core are the common Woo themes of brotherhood, betrayal and the price paid for greed. Woo co-wrote the movie with Patrick Leung and Janet Chun. He then shot it and then edited it. The original cut that played in film festivals around the world was 130 minutes, but it was then whittled to around 100 minutes for its general release. The longer cut was restored for a video release.

The casting of *Bullet in the Head* was particularly good, showcasing some of Hong Kong's best talent.

Jackie Cheung didn't start out wanting to be an actor. Since he has a terrific speaking voice, his friends urged him to enter an amateur singing contest in 1984. He entered and won. Recording deals and movie offers soon followed. It took him only three years to become one of the most popular singers in Hong Kong. His first movie, *Where's Officer Tuba*, was shot in 1986, and he has since made more than thirty movies while continuing to expand his range as a film actor.

Waise Lee was at the opposite end of the artistic scale. He spent years training in an acting school, but could not secure an acting job for years after graduating. He worked at a customs office and occasionally did some modeling on the side. Woo discovered Lee, casting him in a small role opposite Yun-Fat and Ti Lung in *A Better Tomorrow*. Lee then went on to star in such movies as *The Big Heat* (1988), *Spy Games* (1990), and *A Chinese Ghost Story, Part 2* (1990). Woo cast Lee in *Bullet in the Head* because he was confident that Lee could deliver the layered performance required for the role of Paul.

Tony Leung went to the same acting school as Lee (Artiste Training Course in Hong Kong). Upon graduation he immediately started working in television and became a well-known Hong Kong TV star by appearing in such series as *Young Cop* (1980–1982) and *The Deer*. He made his big-screen debut in 1983, but it was Stanley Kwan's *Love Unto Waste* in 1984 that really put him on the map. He won two Best Supporting Actor awards at the Hong Kong Academy Awards for his performances in *People's Hero* in 1986 and for *My Heart Is That Eternal Rose* in 1988. He starred in director Hou Hsiao-hsin's film *City of Sadness* in 1989, which was awarded Best Film at the Venice Film Festival. After *Bullet in the Head*, Leung would work again with Woo in *Hard Boiled* (1992).

Fennie Yuen was only fifteen years old when she was discovered and hired to star in the movie *Happy Ghost II* (1985) in which she was cast as an innocent schoolgirl who encounters a ghost. The movie and Yuen were so well received that she made six similar films in a row. Growing tired of being typecast as a sweet schoolgirl, Yuen decided to risk her career, dramatically shifting gears in 1988 when she accepted Ringo Lam's offer to star in his film *School on Fire* in which she played a student who worked as a prostitute after school. It was a dark and brutal movie that garnered a lot of attention and led to Yuen being asked to join the cast of King Hu's 1990 film *Swordsman* in which she played a nymphomaniac who lived in a room full of venomous snakes. She went directly from that film to *Bullet in the Head*.

While most of the advertising revolved around the three main characters, there was another performance in *Bullet in the Head* that is worthy of note. Actor Simon Yam, the embittered assassin, displays a cool exterior, hiding a badly scarred interior.

In a scene involving one of Yam's hits, Woo shows himself to be a master craftsman. The scene is choreographed to the sounds of the Monkees' tune "I'm a Believer." It is remarkable to watch because there is no dialogue, yet everything is understood as Yam and Leung confront each other in the wake of the killing.

When Woo is asked about the sequence, particularly his choice of music, he responds simply, "I like that song. I like the title: 'I'm a Believer.'"

By the end of the movie Yam's character has atoned for his sins, and is now scarred on the outside but purified within. A blood sacrifice like this is common in Woo movies. Woo's religious beliefs are always evident, but the God he seems to serve in this movie is a harsh one.

When asked about the unrelenting intensity of *Bullet in the Head*, Woo points to his own personal history as well as world history as his influence. "The first half of the movie could be my autobiography. I had the same kinds of friends and I also grew up in the slums. There was a lot of gang fighting and I was always getting beaten up by gangs because I didn't want to join. I was never in a gang. So I had to struggle very hard. We also had a lot of dreams about a better world. What we did have was valuable friendships. I think that the old times were much better than nowadays. The people cared about each other more and looked up to one another more. The new generation seems to be lost. For the second half of the film I was influenced more by the massacre at Tiananmen Square in Beijing in 1989. I was very sad and very upset and felt very ashamed of our country. It was so inhuman to kill all those students. And so I put that pain into the movie, I changed the whole second half of the script—the scenes when they first arrive in Vietnam and they see the students demonstrating. When I shot the movie I almost went crazy because I shot the film with pain. I kept thinking about the tragedy. The original idea for the story didn't have the Vietnam part. I just used it as the future of Hong Kong."

Woo himself saw this as an epic. He filled the movie with a strange mixture of music, everything from the afore-mentioned "I'm a Believer" to more traditional Chinese and Vietnamese music. Lighting styles were also fine-tuned to each scene. Every color seen in each sequence, whether clothing or furniture or walls, was calculated. It was Woo's most technically accomplished piece of work to date, but it was overshadowed by the news that *The Killer* was to be released in North America. *The Killer* would be the first Chinese movie to be released domestically in North America since Bruce Lee's first hit, *Fists of Fury*.

Bullet in the Head didn't grab international audiences the way *The Killer* did, but it did impress other filmmakers and critics. British filmmaker John Boorman (director of *Deliverance* [1972], *Excalibur* [1981]and *The General* [1998], among others) saw the movie on the festival circuit and raved about it. "*Bullet in the Head* is over two hours of remorseless mayhem: balletic deaths, ingenious killings, delightful detonations, rivers of blood, acrobatic fights . . . an explosion of vast energy."

John Powers, film critic for *Vogue*, was completely blown away by *Bullet in the Head*, calling it, "far richer and more moving than *Deer Hunter*—to which it's an answer—this epic of friendship and war in the Saigon of the 1960s has Woo's trademark delirious intensity. Of all his films this one has the greatest sweep and passion."

Barbara Scharres, director of the film center at the Art Institute of Chicago, said, "the riskiest, most challenging Woo film to date. Total appreciation calls for a degree of emotional identification that may not come easily to most Westerners, especially male."

Perhaps one of the most knowing reviews of *Bullet in the Head* was written by critic Ric Meyers, a Hong Kong movie expert who writes for *Inside Hong Kong*. Meyers stated, "The first five minutes of Woo's masterpiece on the nature of brotherhood has more cinematic potency than many entire movies. Tsui Hark tried to undercut Woo with the rushed-out *A Better Tomorrow III*, featuring the contractually straitjacketed Chow Yun-Fat, but Woo's bleak, operatic version remains supreme. Meanwhile, Chow's absence is compensated for by Jackie Cheung's bold, brave performance as the 'title character,' Tony Leung's ability to communicate tragedy, and Waise Lee's wonderful way with the line, 'All I want is this box of gold. Is that so much to ask?'"

After the disappointing box-office results of *Bullet in the Head*, Woo, in an odd move, returned to his romantic-comedy roots. He wanted to make an action-packed romantic comedy and chose to shoot it in Europe. He once again cast Yun-Fat, his alter ego, in the lead role and headed to Paris and the Côte d'Azur to make *Once A Thief* (1990), a movie that he hoped would be a hit. Even though his movies were being critically hailed as brilliant, they were not doing well at the box office and Woo was fearful that he would lose his freedom and clout if he didn't soon make a movie that was a huge financial success.

Hollywood studios gear up for the Christmas season by providing cute-kid movies, big-dog movies, action comedies and a few prestige movies for Oscar consideration. However, in Asia the big festive holiday is the Lunar New Year (known as Chinese New Year), a two-week festival that usually occurs in February. Business shuts down, kids get out of school and families engage in traditional activities, including going to the movies (a recent addition to Chinese tradition). So *Once A Thief* was released during the New Year's festival to hopes of big ticket sales.

Once A Thief follows a trio of art thieves who have made burglary a science and are working the museum circuit in Europe. In the opening sequence, Joe (Yun-Fat), Jim (Leslie Cheung) and Sherry (Cherie Chung) stage a daring heist, stealing a Modigliani from a shipping container while it is in transit from the Louvre to a museum in Nice.

These three were orphans raised by a Fagin-like character named Mr. Chow (Ken Tsang), who trained them to be petty thieves. They quickly advanced, however, into the big time. Stealing great works of art proved to be their most lucrative endeavor. Mr. Chow is also quite happy with their occupation since he takes a cut in return for financing their gigs. The thieves live together in Paris, in a houseboat on the Seine. Jim, the most sensitive of the bunch, has a crush on the exotically beautiful Sherry. Sherry and Joe are involved, even though the callous and chauvinistic Joe treats Sherry very badly. Sherry wants them all to give up burglary. She wants to marry Joe and have a family, but Joe always wants to do "just one last job."

They receive a proposal from Monsieur Le Bond in Nice. He will pay them a huge amount of money if they can steal an obscure painting that is hidden away deep inside a castle on the Côte d'Azur. Sherry has unsettling premonitions that the whole caper will end in disaster, but before she can do anything about it, Jim has already set off. Joe is not worried about Jim's ability, but he is concerned that Jim has struck out on his own. He also knows that Jim has very poor eyesight so he decides to assist him.

The painting is hidden inside a vault in the wine cellar. To reach it, Jim and Joe must get through a series of laser beams, and a network of booby traps. The sequence is quite suspenseful, very funny and ultimately successful, but once they get outside the castle, a gang of armed thugs ambushes them. Jim is shot once as they flee.

The ensuing car chase extends from the top of Mount Bolon to the harbor of Nice, causing all sorts of damage along the way. As they speed along the harbor, a gang of thugs in a speedboat fire on them. Joe turns sharply and rams the car into the speedboat, causing a spectacular crash. Jim survives but Joe is nowhere to be found.

Unbeknownst to Sherry and Jim, Mr. Chow, who would rather see them all dead than retired, has masterminded the whole setup.

Two years later, Sherry has married Jim and his eyesight has grown even worse, so that he is now being reduced to committing petty thefts for Mr. Chow. Then, out of the blue, Joe re-appears. He is handicapped and a changed person. However, his feelings for Sherry haven't changed, making the reunion quite awkward for Jim. But even more than getting back with Sherry, he wants to exact revenge on Mr. Chow who, Joe discovers, was behind the double-cross. So, the three team up once again to stage the biggest heist of all right under Mr. Chow's nose, after which they retire to wealthy yet low-key domesticity in the United States where, in hilarious juxtaposition to their former lives, Sunday afternoon football games, babysitting and household chores dominate.

Woo nabbed his title for *Once A Thief* from a 1965 Ralph Nelson movie of the same name that starred Alain Delon, but Woo's movie doesn't have the same gritty quality as the American film noir movie. Woo's *Once A Thief* owes more to Hitchcock in that the central characters, despite being criminals, remain suave and likable. As well, the comedic aspect is enlightening for those who haven't seen any of Woo's early work. Some very funny material plays over the end credits as Yun-Fat enacts a hilarious depiction of an American domestic scene with a father at home watching football while looking after a baby.

The stunt work in *Once A Thief* is breathtaking. Woo turned to French stunt driver Remy Julien to provide the action required. Julien, like Woo, doesn't know the meaning of the word 'impossible'; there is no stunt that he cannot devise. There is a truly spectacular car chase in this movie that proves that Woo can direct car chases alongside the likes of Peter Yates (*Bullitt*, 1968) and William Friedkin (*French Connection*, 1971, and *To Live and Die in L.A.*, 1984).

The scenes in the castle during a daring art theft are shot with particular deftness and imagination, helping to place *Once A Thief* a cut above similar movies. In 1995 *Mission Impossible* featured a similar infiltration scene that, while exciting, was straightforward, the shots unfolding in a very workman-like way. Woo chooses to make each shot, no matter how inconsequential, count. He also injects humor whenever he thinks he can get away with it, and his judgment is usually sound.

There are moments of heartwrenching poignancy in *Once A Thief*, as a result of the wonderful acting of Yun-Fat. One of these moments shows Joe revealing that he is in fact still alive, although confined to a wheelchair. The scene waits for the emotional impact before commencing any dialogue. Another terrific moment comes at a charity ball during which Joe dances with Sherry despite being wheelchair bound. Yun-Fat is impressive as he gracefully maneuvers the wheelchair. Woo shoots the scene from several angles in slow-motion. It is a lovely sequence. As a finishing touch the action-packed ending of the movie is not only visually spectacular but also charming and funny.

Production company Golden Princess had pressured Woo to provide a more upbeat ending for the movie. The movie ends with three lives at crossroads, three people who know that the glory days are over. Woo downplays this. "I have a script but no storyboards. I just work from day to day and if I or someone else have a better idea than the one I had before, then I put it in. Originally the ending was going to be more like *Casablanca*, but we changed it completely before we were finished."

As good as it is, *Once A Thief* never really gels the way Woo's previous movies do. But when compared with a Hollywood offering like *Hudson Hawk* (1991), a similarly themed movie starring Bruce Willis, it is a downright masterpiece.

When *Once A Thief* started playing the festival circuit it was accepted with positive reaction across the board. Howard Hampton wrote of *Once A Thief*, "It feels like nothing so much as a Hope-Crosby-Lamour version of *Beat the Devil*, in which gunfire is just a form of snappy patter. And has anyone been more debonair in a wheel-chair than Chow Yun-Fat?" Woo's version of *Once A Thief*, (the full version,) previewed at the Toronto International Festival of Festivals.

After *Once A Thief*, Woo would make one more film in Hong Kong before heading off to Hollywood. That movie was *Hard Boiled*, a movie that would leave action audiences breathless.

Six

1992:
ONE DOOR CLOSES,
ANOTHER SWINGS OPEN

"I choreograph action like you'd design a dancing sequence in a musical. I have a sense of beauty and the rhythm of the action, the atmosphere and the action's emotional arch. Everything is clear in my mind before I shoot. But, like a musical, the rhythm and movement have to be filmed as precisely as you've thought it out."

JOHN WOO

Two Hong Kong detectives go into a teahouse for some breakfast after a night at a jazz bar, as part of an undercover operation aimed at ferreting out illegal gunrunners.

The tension builds as the two detectives joke about leaving Hong Kong in '97. Suddenly, the tougher looking of the two springs into action when he realizes that the gunrunners are in the teahouse. What follows is a stunning gunfight involving machine guns, pistols, an army of mobsters, two fierce detectives and a platoon of uniformed Hong Kong cops. The sequence ends with a man-to-man confrontation between the surviving detective and the lead crook that ends with startling finality. This is the first action sequence in Woo's last Hong Kong-made movie, *Hard Boiled* (1992). It was the first in an unbelievable number of action scenes in a movie that is truly breathtaking in its bombast. *Hard Boiled* went on to overtake *The Killer* as Woo's international calling card.

Hard Boiled was a big movie in the Hong Kong sense. The movie took a lengthy 123 days to shoot (Woo had only sixty-five days to shoot the Hollywood film *Hard Target* in 1993) and it was loaded with stunts. Woo was enthusiastic, as he was finally in a position to really enjoy making a movie, no longer laboring under the oppressive pressure of having to succeed. His name, when connected to an action movie that starred Chow Yun-Fat, virtually guaranteed something spectacular. He loved the story line, "Hong Kong criminals have gone too far now," said Woo at the time. "We need a guy to go up against them and this is Chow Yun-Fat's character. It's called *Hard*

Boiled because that is the term given to [a] tough kind of detective novel. I try for a similar kind of 'hard boiled' style in this film."

While he was shooting the movie he described it as "*Dirty Harry* meets *Die Hard* with a little bit of *Miami Vice* thrown in for good measure." Yun-Fat was also enjoying himself immensely. When asked about the movie at the time he grinned broadly and said, "This movie is 70 percent action and 30 percent story." Yun-Fat was also frank when asked about the believability of the movie—"In America a policeman must shout 'stop!' before shooting someone. Over here [Hong Kong] you can shoot anytime you want, without warning."

A dissenting opinion of the movie and of Woo's direction came from one of the lead actors, Anthony Wong, who played Johnny, the central villain in *Hard Boiled*. He found the movie far too comic book-like and wasn't pleased with the way Woo directed the actors. "We didn't have any communications at all. He doesn't really trust actors . . . except Chow Yun-Fat."

The opening sequence is a mind-blower. Yun-Fat, at his coolest, plays a plainclothes detective named Tequila who moonlights in a jazz bar, playing the clarinet. His drummer is a fellow cop named Lionheart (played by Bowie Lam). After a night of music and gin, Tequila goes for an early morning dim sum at the Wyndham Teahouse, a famous Hong Kong landmark where the customers bring their own caged birds to sing while they are eating. It is a large teahouse and often very crowded. On this morning, a bunch of gunrunning gangsters are holding a meeting. These gangsters have hidden guns in the false bottoms of their birdcages. Tequila makes a move on them and a gun battle erupts in the crowded restaurant. Birds scatter in all directions as the bullets—thousands of them—fly. Lionheart takes several bullets and dies. Tequila goes ballistic, taking out criminals left, right and center. In what has become a famous sequence, Tequila slides down a banister with a toothpick clenched in his teeth, two guns blazing, chases a gunman into the kitchen, leaps onto a counter, gets covered in flour and blasts the gunman at close range, splattering himself with blood.

As the story unfolds we are introduced to Tony (Tony Leung) who is a well-dressed, swaggering killer working for a mob boss named Hoi. Tony is an underworld golden boy and Hoi's chief rival, a young lunatic gunrunner named Johnny (Anthony Wong), covets his services. Johnny also wants Hoi's rackets and, in a daring attack in a warehouse, tries to take them. Here Woo introduces eye-popping cinematic techniques and every imaginable firearm. Johnny's main henchman, Mad Dog (Kuo Chui), mows down legions of Hoi's men single-handedly before a standoff between Hoi and Johnny halts the action.

Meanwhile, in another part of the warehouse, Tequila lies in wait. The battle ends with Tony and Tequila pointing guns at each other's heads. Tequila pulls the trigger—his gun is empty. Rather than killing Tequila, Tony lets him go. As it turns out, Tony is also an undercover cop, who has infiltrated this mob of arms smugglers. He is so deeply involved that he doesn't seem to mind committing contract murders for his boss to keep his assumed persona intact. But this does have a psychological effect on Tony. After each hit he constructs origami figures, which he then hangs throughout his houseboat.

As Tequila and Tony come to understand each other's involvement, they also discover the whereabouts of Johnny's massive arsenal. It is hidden away in a high-tech basement storage facility, concealed in the basement of Maple Group Hospital.

This hospital sets the stage for the finale of the movie. And it plays out in such an orgy of stylish action that it requires several viewings to absorb it all. Just when the action reaches a zenith in ferocity, Woo serves up yet another unbelievable set piece that takes place in the hospital's maternity ward. These outrageous scenes were shot in a new studio that was called "The Coca-Cola Factory," since the studio was formerly a Coke bottling plant. (Incidentally, if you take a look at the film *Heroic Trio* (1993) you will recognize Woo's sets for *Hard Boiled*. They were used almost unchanged.)

With the assistance of a policewoman named Teresa (played with relish by comedienne Teresa Mo), Tequila sees to it that the ward full of babies is taken to safety while all around them rages a firefight of epic proportions.

The movie takes a turn towards the humorously surreal while Tequila is seeing to the safety of the last of the babies, a round-faced little tyke with the unlikely name of Saliva Sammy. Tequila tucks cotton balls in Sammy's ears to protect him from the "X-rated action" that is raging all around them. Tequila holds little Sammy under one arm while blasting away at Johnny's legion of "killable dogs" with the other. Just before they reach the window where Sammy is to be lowered to safety, an explosion rips through the hallway, igniting Tequila's pant leg. Lucky for Tequila he has got Sammy in tow, because at precisely the right moment Sammy pees down Tequila's leg, putting out the fire. Tequila and Saliva Sammy make it safely to the parking lot below just before the arms cache explodes, lighting up the sky.

Moments of humor like the extinguished-fire scene are not out of place in Woo films. Woo often peppers his movies, even the most action packed, with humorous moments. Earlier in *Hard Boiled*, Tequila is complaining about not having a suitable place to live, saying that he makes too much money for subsidized housing, but doesn't make near enough for a nice apartment. One of his cohorts tells him that he should move into the jazz bar where he will at least get "a lot of sax."

Woo pulls a Hitchcock or a Scorsese by actually appearing in *Hard Boiled,* but takes it one step further by playing Mr. Woo, the bartender/owner of the jazz bar.

As good as *Hard Boiled* is (it is perhaps one of the best shoot-'em-up action movies ever made), it's not without flaws. For example, Woo tries to be too stylish. This movie lays it on so thick that the camera tricks and cinematic techniques start to obscure the story. Of course, the same can be said of such masterpieces as Francis Ford Coppola's *Apocalypse Now* (1979)—unarguably a piece of cinematic art, but made even richer by the presence of its flaws. The flaws add a grittiness and a realism. Many film critics who watch the Hong Kong film industry closely consider the movie worthy of enthusiastic recommendation, but not worthy of a ten-best list.

Barbara Scharres, director of the Film Center at the School of the Art Institute of Chicago, and a frequent commentator on the Hong Kong film scene for *Film Comment, Variety* and *American Cinematographer* said, "The film became Woo's showpiece in the West while providing closure on his career in Hong Kong. For once his spectacular action seems to signify a state of endless purgatory rather than a consummation of passion."

Los Angeles film reviewer Andy Klein writes of *Hard Boiled,* "John Woo's last Hong Kong film is almost a distillation of his post-1986 work. Even if the plot is full of holes, and the emotional tug isn't quite as strong as in *The*

Killer, the action sequences (nearly the whole movie) are among the greatest ever filmed."

Mainstream American critics were taken in by the action and that aspect of the movie was the focal point of many reviews. *The Los Angeles Times* wrote, "With *Hard Boiled* John Woo shows himself to be the best director of contemporary action films working anywhere." *The Hollywood Reporter* wrote that *Hard Boiled* "blows away most action films in recent memory." And the *New York Daily News* enthused, "*Hard Boiled* is an action film's dream. It takes viewers straight through the roof and out of this world."

Andy Klein's point about the plot being full of holes is valid. But Woo washes the screen with such an unbelievable array of stunts and action sequences we don't have time to question the validity of what is going on—until the movie is over. James Cameron has often been singled out for similarly hoodwinking the audience with such razzle dazzle that we don't really question the sheer nonsense of many of his movie plots.

As *Hard Boiled* headed into production, *Once A Thief* started making the rounds at film festivals. By now, cinephiles the world over knew Woo's name and his work, and they were anxiously awaiting anything new from him.

Once A Thief was a bit of a shock to the more recent Woo fans who knew his reputation as a major action man, a Hong Kong reincarnation of Sam Peckinpah. But *Once*

A Thief was actually a return to the genre he knew best, adventure-comedy. Despite the quiet success of *Once A Thief* Woo shrewdly recognized that his new audience was expecting high-octane set pieces, like those in *The Killer* and *Hard Boiled*.

In September of 1992, the Toronto International Festival of Festivals—currently known as the Toronto International Film Festival—had featured the North American premiere of Woo's *Hard Boiled*. Also shown was Quentin Tarantino's gritty first film *Reservoir Dogs*. Tarantino's film contained several obvious homages and tributes to the Hong Kong action films of John Woo and Ringo Lam. During several interviews Tarantino gave during the Toronto festival, he would waxed enthusiastically about the work of Woo. Tarantino played a very real role in getting younger, hipper journalists to notice Woo.

Woo had been to the Toronto Festival of Festivals a number of times, and on this occasion he was pleasantly surprised and intrigued by the hero worship he was receiving from the young filmmaker who was attracting such attention himself. The presence of these two mercurial talents on the movie scene at the same festival was too good an opportunity to pass up.

Meetings between Woo and Tarantino were hastily put together in hotel rooms and restaurants, and agents and producers started hinting that a deal of some kind was in the works. For Woo, the chance to sit down with Tarantino presented, if not an open door, at least a view to the Hollywood scene.

The announcement from William Morris stated that Woo and Tarantino had "finalized" an agreement to collaborate on their first project together. The untitled project was described as an action thriller to be set in Los Angeles and Hong Kong that would be written by Tarantino based on an original idea, and directed by Woo. The movie was to star an internationally known Asian leading man (Yun-Fat) and a prominent American actor.

Interestingly, the announcement listed as producers of this intended movie Terence Chang, Woo's long-time friend and producing partner; Jim Jacks and Sean Daniel, who would later produce Woo's American debut *Hard Target* (1993); and Tarantino and his producing partner Lawrence Bender. The senior vice president, and co-head of William Morris Picture Department, Mike Simpson and William Morris agents Lee Stollman and Christopher Godsick brokered the agreement. Godsick would later leave the William Morris Agency to help form WCG Productions (Woo, Chang and Godsick). Simpson was quoted as saying that Tarantino and Woo have a "deep-felt admiration for each other's work; Quentin's terrific idea and the script he will write, along with John's ability to present compelling characters with incredible action sequences were the elements that fused this creative link."

Tarantino would eventually develop something of a treatment but Woo wasn't very excited by it. It contained several major gunfights but very little story development. Woo's films, while they are accented with violence and action, are by and large about brotherhood and loyalty and betrayal. Woo remarked to someone at the time that he felt that Tarantino simply "didn't get it." They both moved on to their own separate projects with the hope that they might once again try to forge that creative link.

After *Hard Boiled*, neither Woo nor his alter ego Yun-Fat would ever be the same. Woo decided to leave Hong Kong for phase two of his excellent adventure while Chow Yun-Fat would remain in Hong Kong to make a few more movies, including the brilliant *Full Contact* (1992) for director Ringo Lam, in which he plays an action scene that would have made even maestro John Woo green with envy. The sequence features a gunfight shown from the bullet's point of view, with the camera following the bullet from the barrel of the gun to the target. Woo and Yun-Fat were both already very successful men but they were itching for change. Both would choose Hollywood as the venue for their expansionist plans.

In Hong Kong, the announcement that Woo was making the move to Hollywood prompted a widespread wave of speculation as to the real reasons he was leaving, especially since he was at the pinnacle of his success. One explanation that seemed to be given the most credence was that

Woo was fleeing from the tyranny of the triad-controlled film industry. Woo denies this: "The triads know me pretty well," he said. "They know I'm tough and I'm always over budget. I spend too much money to be a good investment for them, so I never really had them knocking on my door."

When Woo talks about his decision to move to Los Angeles, he again spreads around the credit. "Terence Chang set up everything for me here," says Woo. "He brought *The Killer* to all the festivals and made all the calls. I am so appreciative of my partner. When I decided to make the move to L.A. it was because of him. And it was a good decision to make."

Seven

1993–1994:
THE YELLOW BRICK ROAD

"I would never even allow myself to dream that I could make movies in Hollywood."

JOHN WOO

After making *Hard Boiled* Woo could no longer resist the lure of Hollywood. By 1993, it was time to make the move, because he had a savvy partner in Terence Chang, and several offers of meetings with studio executives. When your name gets a certain amount of attention, it is best to take advantage quickly because, in Hollywood, attention fades fast. Woo was still an unproven entity in Los Angeles, but his reputation preceded him. Woo and Chang were in a fortunate position, but they wanted to be careful. Take their time. And only commit to a project they were comfortable with. They would sift through dozens of screenplays and a myriad of offers before settling on a script called *Hard Target* (1993).

As a byproduct of the huge success of his Hong Kong movies on the festival circuit and on video, it was virtually certain that Hollywood would attempt to remake some of Woo's films, taking advantage of his growing popularity.

Woo conceded that working in Hong Kong, where the government controls all aspects of the artistic process, scared him a bit. But he insists that this was not the main factor behind his decision. He says that he liked the pace of working in America much more, the working hours were a big draw. These considerations would mean he could spend a lot more time with his family, something that his wife had criticized him about for years.

Chang, having been Woo's business partner for three years, had also quietly established himself as a major influence in the Hong Kong film industry and now was becoming internationally known. But the route he had taken in becoming an important producer/manager had been a circuitous one. Chang, having a keen interest in shape and design, studied at the University of Oregon where he earned a degree in architecture. He developed an interest in filmmaking during the mid-seventies when the industry seemed to be exploding. Chang was interested not so much in the blockbuster movies coming out of Hollywood but rather in the films being made by New

York directors like Martin Scorsese. Chang enrolled in the New York University film school to see just how deep his interest was.

In 1978, Chang returned to Hong Kong where he applied his newfound enthusiasm and NYU experience to his own film industry. He joined Golden Harvest, where he served as production manager for two forgettable films (*Itchy Fingers* [1979] and *Game of Death II* [1979]) before joining producer Johnny Mak and his Johnny Mak Productions in 1981. It was an upward move for Chang because at Johnny Mak Productions, Chang was finally given the chance to produce movies outright. He produced *Lonely 15* (1981), *Dragon Force* (1982) and *Everlasting Love* (1983). *Everlasting Love* was selected to participate in the Director's Fortnight program at the Cannes Film Festival in 1984.

Chang left Johnny Mak Productions in 1986 to join forces with the much-larger D&B Films. There he was placed in charge of the international distribution arm of the company where he helped launch the international careers of such stars as Brandon Lee, son of martial-arts legend Bruce Lee, who was tragically killed in an accident on the set of his 1994 breakout film *The Crow*; Michelle Khan (who also uses the name Michelle Yeoh), Jackie Chan's co-star in *Supercop* (1996) and co-star of *Tomorrow Never Dies* (1997) opposite Pierce Brosnan as James Bond; and American martial-arts B-movie superstar Cynthia Rothrock.

In 1988, Chang continued his upward momentum by joining Hong Kong's Cinema Workshop, when he was installed in the position of General Manager. While working there, he oversaw production of and international marketing of such films as *Gunmen* (1988) and *Chinese Ghost Story 2* (1990).

In 1990 Chang teamed up with his favorite director, Woo, and producer Linda Kuk to form Milestone Pictures, an independent production company. The company would produce *Once A Thief* and *Hard Boiled*.

Chang's reputation as a terrific middleman led to his becoming a manager almost without consciously deciding to be a manager. Apart from all his other jobs, he continues to successfully manage the careers of Chow Yun-Fat and the prolific writer Lillian Lee, whose books include *Rouge* and *The Last Princess of Manchuria*.

Woo and Chang were inundated with scripts from Hollywood studios and producers. Woo says, "Some of them were good—some of them were very good—but the rest were simply martial-arts movies, and I told the producers that I had no interest in doing those kinds of films anymore. I'd done a lot of them already."

Ironically, one of the projects presented to Woo at this time was a script called *Face/Off*, a movie that he would make in 1997. Woo turned the script down flat because, at the time, *Face/Off* was more of a science-fiction picture than an action movie. He remembers his thoughts on the project, "I never liked futuristic movies much, so there was absolutely no interest in it for that reason. Beyond that, even if I took the job because I wanted to be in Hollywood that badly, I was sure I could not do a good job on a film like that."

One actor who desperately wanted to work with Woo in Hollywood was Brandon Lee. Lee had made a TV movie sequel to the *Kung Fu* television series. Then, when no feature offers were forthcoming at home, he headed to Germany where he accepted an offer to star in a completely forgettable movie called *Laser Mission* (1990). Discouraged at the direction that his career was going and constantly barraged with questions about his famous father Bruce Lee, Lee took acting classes.

About being the son of the legendary Bruce Lee, he said, "I can't pretend that it's been anything other than a positive thing, and it's brought me opportunities that I might not otherwise have had. However, it would be completely ridiculous to try to be like him on film. We grew up in different countries and spoke different languages. We are different men." That said, Lee did go the route that his father took when his career stalled in Hollywood—he headed to Hong Kong to make a film there. He hoped for a film that would be stylish, with enough action to impress Hollywood producers. The film Lee accepted in Hong Kong was *Legacy of Rage* (1986), and the results were as he had hoped. *Legacy of Rage* was a cut above most action movies and he parlayed that film into a role opposite Dolph Lundgren in the Warner Bros. film *Showdown in Little Tokyo* (1991). Lee was then approached by Twentieth Century Fox to enter into a multi-picture arrangement with them. The first film was to be called *Rapid Fire* (1992). Lee desperately wanted Woo to direct *Rapid Fire* (Terence Chang had arranged for Brandon Lee to make *Legacy of Rage* in Hong Kong). The deal for Woo to direct *Rapid Fire* came close to being signed, but eventually the studio wanted a martial-arts action movie rather than the kind of movie that Woo was interested in making. The movie was eventually made in 1992 by director Dwight Little and, at the time, it was called "the best Hong Kong movie ever made in America."

Another American star who was very interested in working with John Woo was Jeff Speakman. Speakman, a tall, handsome martial artist scored a surprise hit with his 1991 Paramount release *The Perfect Weapon*. Speakman knew that to consolidate his popularity he needed to follow it up with an even better movie. He asked Woo to consider working with him on something, but Woo politely declined citing the usual reason—he was uninterested in making more martial-arts movies.

Chang accepted Universal Pictures' offer, making *Hard Target* the first movie Woo would direct for a Hollywood studio. It was Universal chairman Tom

Pollock who decided to make the offer in the first place. He did so after seeing *The Killer*, but he made the offer with a warning—one that should have set off alarm bells—tone down the violence and reduce the body count.

Universal Pictures, who had a multi-picture arrangement with Jean-Claude Van Damme, saw *Hard Target* as a potential vehicle for their star. Van Damme was thrilled. He was a huge fan of Woo's films, and had arranged to meet with him in Hong Kong. Van Damme recalls, "My English was not so good and his English was not so good but we had a few drinks together and after a while we seemed to be communicating on a level that was beyond language, almost like telepathy."

Woo was interested in making *Hard Target*, regardless of Van Damme's involvement. After meeting with the actor Woo had second thoughts. "Van Damme wanted some changes," says Woo. "He wanted to prove himself as a serious actor and he thought this movie might do it for him if he was able to dictate certain things early on." Woo was fairly keen on the project and felt that it was time he committed to a Hollywood movie. Also, when he questioned himself about doing the movie he was able to come up with all the right answers. "I know myself," states Woo. "I'm pretty sure of my abilities and I know how to make an actor look good on screen, make him look like a hero. I thought I could do the same for Van Damme." At the time Woo was actively pursuing actor Kurt Russell for the lead role, but Russell was booked solid for two years to come, so Woo turned to Van Damme.

Woo's search for a Hollywood vehicle to sink his teeth into was proving discouraging. If the scripts weren't for martial-arts movies, they were full of violence and gunfights, but lacking soul and story—just violence for its own sake. When Woo read a screenplay given to him by Chuck Pfarrer, he was genuinely hopeful, "Chuck Pfarrer did a good job with the script for *Hard Target*," Woo says. "It is a simple but powerful story, with a lot of feeling underneath. For a good action film you need a solid structure. Chuck gave me that."

Hard Target was to be yet another variation on the themes explored in *The Most Dangerous Game*, the 1932 movie released by RKO in which Joel McCrae played a mad hunter who lures guests onto his island so he can hunt them down like animals.

Hard Target opens with a homeless man who is running for his life in the dark. Men pursue him with guns, on foot and on motorcycles. The frightened homeless man is finally brought down by steel-tipped arrows fired from a crossbow by a marksman who has paid a handsome sum of money for the privilege of hunting down a man and killing him in cold blood. The prey (played by writer Chuck Pfarrer) has been chosen by an ice-cold criminal, Fouchon (Lance Henriksen), who runs a business that supplies human prey for well-heeled hunters looking for the ultimate in hunting thrills.

Fouchon and his assistant Van Cleaf (Arnold Vosloo) choose only homeless combat veterans with no families for their nefarious game. Things start to come apart when the wrong homeless man is sent out on a hunt and his daughter Natasha (Yancy Butler) comes looking for her missing father. She is a stranger in New Orleans and the victim of a near mugging her first day in the city. She escapes with the help of a Cajun merchant marine named Chance Boudreaux (Jean-Claude Van Damme). Since Chance needs to earn $217 quickly to pay some union dues, he accepts Natasha's offer of a short-term private investigator's job to help her find her father. Chance finds his way to Fouchon and Van Cleaf and forces them into the deadliest hunt of their careers. The movie ends with a huge gun battle involving Chance, about a hundred mercenaries, Natasha and Chance's old bootlegging Uncle Duvet (Wilford Brimley).

This union between Woo and Universal Pictures was not an agreeable one right off the bat. Producer Jim Jacks remembers that getting Universal to even consider Woo required "a difficult period of convincing." Once Woo was hired he quickly won everybody over, although he was still a bit nervous at the mandate to tone down the violent aspects of the film. He honestly did not understand why he would be allowed to make the film at all if he was to be constantly restrained. "In my Hong Kong films my heroes can be just as ruthless as my villains," says Woo. "But here [Hollywood] if the villain and the hero confront one another and the villain runs out of bullets, the hero cannot shoot him unless the villain picks up a knife or a club."

Jacks recalls that Woo "was not the most powerful person on the set but as far as I was concerned, he was certainly the most respected." Lance Henriksen recalls that it took only a short while before everyone connected with the project started thinking of the movie as a "John Woo movie rather than a Jean-Claude Van Damme movie." Indeed, the actors seemed to be responding favorably to this unique opportunity of working with a filmmaker in transition, and were very open to his direction. In one scene near the end of the movie Henriksen's character's long, black cashmere coat is set alight. Henriksen continues to act even though flames are shooting up his back and over his head. If you look closely at the sequence you will see that Henriksen's hair and back have been soaked down with fire-retardant chemicals, but that doesn't diminish the impact of the scene.

The pairing of Van Damme and Woo proved to be a reasonable one, despite Woo's early misgivings. Van Damme is trained in dance and is an excellent martial artist. In fact, after Woo watched Van Damme rehearse some of the fighting scenes he immediately redesigned some of the fights to make them even more spectacular, as he knew that Van Damme was up to it.

For the Belgian-born Van Damme, this was also a pairing made in cinema heaven. A Belgian actor and a Hong Kong director in a Hollywood movie—"This is why I love America," says Van Damme, "anything is possible." About Woo, Van Damme is equally ebullient, "I knew from the beginning that John Woo would be a wonderful director for me. He is great with action, of course, but what I notice is that he is very good with actors. He always makes his actors look good."

Being that *Hard Target* was Woo's first film shot in America, he had to be very patient when communicating with his crew. Often, when he could not adequately articulate his directions, he would resort to such statements as "this will be the Sam Peckinpah shot" so that his cinematographer would get the general idea of what he was trying to achieve. He was ultimately very grateful to his helpful American crew. "Making movies in America, I feel like dreams can come true. Anything I can imagine, any shot, any action I think of, they can do. They always tried to give me what I wanted." says Woo.

What he wanted in his American debut was action, lots of action. To help him he turned to a crack team of stunt and weapons people. Authenticity was an early concern. *Hard Target* contained several nerve-wracking action sequences, which meant putting star Van Damme in harm's way. To avoid an accident Woo enlisted the help of his screenwriter Chuck Pfarrer and stuntman Mark Stefanich. Stefanich was brought in as Van Damme's principal stunt double and he and Pfarrer, who had served together in the Navy SEALs, put the actors through their paces on how trained men stalk other men, and how to use high-tech weaponry.

While in the SEALs Stefanich perfected a trick he called the "flying reload" for slamming a new magazine in his automatic pistol or machine gun while he was running or leaping through the air. He taught the actors this technique so they were able to maintain their pace without throwing credibility out the window during every action scene. Pfarrer was proud of the results: "This is one movie where you will never be able to scoff at how many bullets they fire on one clip. You'll see them reload when they need to."

One particular gunfight features a neat little trick that Woo incorporated into the movie after watching Stefanich give an on-set weapons demonstration. It involves a semi-automatic pistol held upside down while fanning the trigger with the index finger, creating a rapid-fire machine-gun sound.

Woo's relationship with guns is a curious one. He treats guns as components to his scenes, almost like characters in their own right. Woo spends a lot of time listening to the sounds of gunfire during the editing process and he tinkers with it constantly. Woo describes it this way: "The sounds of the guns in a film like *The Killer* are created by putting the sounds of several guns on top of each other." Chuck Pfarrer confirms this attention to detail: "John really cares about all these little things. That is part of what sets his work apart. When the shell casing hits the floor, it even sounds like the right kind of metal, like brass sounds when it hits the floor. That is a unique sound. No one who ever hears such a sound in that context is ever likely to forget it."

Gun expert Robert "Rock" Galotti remembered his first taste of working with Woo. (Galotti subsequently worked on *Broken Arrow* (1996) and *Face/Off* (1997) with Woo.) "No matter how big the gun sounds were on *Hard Target*, John always wanted them bigger."

Some of the weapons fire necessitated the design of new forms of protection for the crew. Woo likes to use full powder loads in his gunfire sequences and, because he likes to move the camera around, the regular shields set up next to the camera postions to protect the camera operators weren't sufficent. A new bulletproof Plexiglass shield was devised that could be bolted right to the camera. This was particularly useful in one sequence that has Jean-Claude Van Damme emptying a clip of ammo right into the camera.

The New Orleans location provided many wonderful visuals, but added almost as many difficulties. One major sequence was scheduled to be shot in the famed French Quarter, a historic region and popular tourist attraction. Movie scenes involving gunfire and explosions were a first for this area of the city and city officials obviously were not fully aware of what the phrase "action sequence" meant on a Woo movie set. The French Quarter was rigged with thousands of "squibs" (small explosive charges that simulate a bullet hit) and thousands more rounds were ignited.

Cinematographer Russell Carpenter faced a major challenge when filming a huge gunfight in an old warehouse used to store garish floats used in the Mardi Gras parade. Carpenter remembers, "Just the lighting of a space like that, with all those strange shapes and shadows was difficult enough, but John then added the further complication of wanting the scene shot from several angles at once—often with more than one of the cameras moving." Carpenter was quite impressed with the planning and preparation Woo brought to the set of *Hard Target*, "He uses it all. He lays down three dolly tracks at once, or he shoots an exploding truck with seven different cameras rolling at once. You can bet that every one of those angles will be used when the scene is finally cut together."

Producer Jim Jacks firmly supported Woo's shooting style. "It may look a little extravagant to have four or five cameras rolling at once, but it's actually the most economical way to shoot a John Woo-type action picture. Those additional cameras aren't for added coverage, they are separate angles—the equivalent of another setup."

When it came time to edit the footage, incorporating all of these angles, editor Bob Murawski was up to the task. He had been working on a state-of-the-art computerized editing unit that allowed him to edit material as the movie was being shot. He too was impressed and grateful when it came to Woo's style of shooting. "A lot of directors just shoot, almost at random, leaving this mass of footage that we then have to hack and carve into a scene. With John, I'm never in doubt about what he intended with each sequence. One of his sequences has 357 cuts in it—and every one of them was in his head before he started shooting. His footage just melts together."

Stunts proved to be problematic. Stunt coordinator Billy Burton rigged a head-on crash involving a motorcycle and a Jeep 4x4, which, according to Burton, had never been attempted on film before. In the scene, Van Damme's character astride the motorcycle races towards the Jeep with guns blazing. He then jumps on the seat of the speeding motorcycle and rides it like a surfboard before the motorcycle crashes into the Jeep. The crash sends Chance over the Jeep and onto the road behind it. It was that kind of stunt work Woo was hoping to include in his first American movie, but there is a limit to what the ratings board, the Motion Picture Association of America, would accept. Much to Woo's chagrin he was about to clash with the other side of Hollywood moviemaking.

Throughout the shooting of *Hard Target*, Woo felt the constraints of studio moviemaking tightening around him. His last Hong Kong action movie, *Hard Boiled*, was shot in 123 days. Universal Pictures insisted that *Hard Target* be shot in only sixty-five days, which put him under tremendous pressure. Woo's last few Hong Kong movies allowed him almost complete autonomy over every aspect of the process. Yet, in Hollywood he quickly had to get used to the studio executives watching over his shoulder constantly. When asked about the first noticeable difference between making movies in Hollywood and Hong Kong, he chuckles and says, "Meetings. They like to have a lot of meetings about everything, they have meetings to decide when the next meeting will be. In Hong Kong we have one meeting to decide how much money we need, and that's it." Jim Jacks elaborates, "John wasn't used to having input from so many others into his movies. I always felt that his English got better or worse depending on how much he disliked what he was being told. If he didn't like it, it got really bad."

Actor Chow Yun-Fat visited his friend on the New Orleans set and was immediately taken by the differences. "They told him that, if he shoots five people in this scene, then he can only shoot two people in the next scene." Chow shakes his head as he remembers, "John was told that he could not kill seven people in this scene and then another seven in the scene right after that."

Woo had hoped that Jean-Claude Van Damme's significant martial-arts skills would help make up the difference. Fans of Woo's movies were accustomed to big gunfights with numerous casualties. Perhaps a few dazzling hand-to-hand combat scenes might bridge the gap imposed by the ratings board. But even that proved problematic. Universal Pictures, for its part, was not sure an Asian director, specifically this Asian director, could handle the rigors of American moviemaking and the large American crews. Big action movies require a lot of on-set communication, and they didn't see the quiet, gentlemanly Woo with his limited command of English as someone who could coordinate such a large-scale project. Universal hired Sam Raimi (director of *Evil Dead* (1983) and *Darkman* (1990) among others) to oversee the production. Raimi is a die-hard Woo fan, and his enthusiasm was part of the reason that Universal selected him for the job. Raimi was delighted to be able to hang out with Woo, the maestro, on the set of his first American picture and get paid for it. Enthusiasm for Woo's work put him on the set, but Universal also wanted a proven director on standby should Woo fail them. Raimi argued with the studio, saying, "Woo at 70 percent is still going to blow away most American action directors working at 100 percent!" Writer Chuck Pfarrer made a similar observation when

Hard Target was released: "I wouldn't like to be an American director with a buddy-cop action movie coming out this summer, because there is a new sheriff in town and his name is John Woo."

Once the film was made, edited and scored (a terrific soundtrack by Graeme Revell featuring the Kodo drummers of Japan), the real battle began. Woo was contractually obligated to deliver for release to Universal Pictures an R-rated film, meaning it could be action-packed but must be suitable for a teenaged audience. When the movie was submitted to the MPAA, they judged it too violent and too intense and slapped an NC-17 rating on it. This rating is tantamount to an X-rating. Blockbuster Video, the monolithic video chain that has all but devoured the mom-and-pop video stores, will not carry an NC-17 film on its shelves. Some newspapers and television stations will not run ads for an NC-17 rated movie. Getting an NC-17 rating can take a significant bite from the ticket sales. It was also something that Woo did not expect, but it was not unprecedented in his career. In 1973 Woo's first movie, *The Young Dragons*, was so violent that the Hong Kong motion picture ratings board had a difficult time with it. It was eventually released without being cut, but it took some explaining on Woo's part to justify the problematic scenes. When *The Killer* was released in North America the MPAA wasn't thrilled with the body count there either.

Cuts were ordered for *Hard Target*, a film that expended more than 25,000 rounds of ammunition. Woo cut the film and re-submitted it. He was forced to re-cut the film again . . . and again . . . and again, eight times until it finally was awarded an R-rating. During this editing, Van Damme requested and received a print of the film that he attempted to edit on his own, but the result was so ludicrous it inspired howls of laughter. Van Damme had excised whole characters to insert more close-ups of himself. When asked about this, Van Damme angrily retorted, "People pay their money to see me, not to see Lance Henriksen."

Jim Jacks remembers Woo bemusedly going back into the editing room, time and time again, wondering why he was hired by a Hollywood studio in the first place if he was going to be asked to trim out all of the elements that distinguished him as a filmmaker.

"I don't think it was the amount of blood that the MPAA had a problem with; I think it was the number of deaths," said Jacks. Writer Chuck Pfarrer was on Woo's side, "Poor guy, this was all new to him. In Hong Kong he can shoot whatever he wants and they will release it and generally audiences will go and see it and decide for themselves if it is any good or not. Here he was put in the position of having his abilities and his vision second guessed by people who had the power but who had no vision or ability of their own." That pretty much summed up the problem faced by Woo in this ratings battle. Since he had never encountered this kind of ratings system before, he was already at a disadvantage when it came to this bureaucracy. The MPAA told him to make cuts, and told him that the film was too violent, but they never indicated exactly what it was they found objectionable. Woo remembers, "We were really doing the cutting just by guessing what they wanted or what they didn't want. By the sixth time when one of them told me, 'I don't like violence,' I got mad and said to him, 'If you don't like the violence, don't go to the movie.' They really don't care about your purpose, what your real idea is, they just say 'too violent.'"

In the end Woo was forced to make twenty cuts to his movie to qualify for the rating he needed. The opening sequence, in which the hunters pursue the homeless man, required seven cuts. The first was a four-second close-up showing Binder agonizingly removing an arrow from his shoulder. This was a bit too gratuitous for the MPAA. The next cut came when Binder runs to a house to seek help. Shots blast into the house all around him, and a steel arrow whizzes past him and through a window. The cut is six seconds long and really defies reasoning other than perhaps that the editing was altering the pace of the sequence, and the cut was made for timing purposes. The next cut was the longest made—a fifteen-second cut that showed Binder throwing a gas-filled can at an attacker on a motorcycle. The can and the motorcycle explode in flames and the rider is killed. Again, it was deemed excessively violent. Binder is eventually hit with three arrows from a high-powered crossbow, but we only see two. The second arrow hits him in the buttock. That eight-second scene was cut. As Binder struggles to get to his feet on a bridge Woo made a one-second cut of his shaky legs. The next one-second cut is a freeze frame of a third arrow (the kill shot) hitting Binder. The last cut of this sequence was a three-second scene showing Binder floating in the water.

The rest of the cuts were to the big gunfight scene at the end of the movie in the Mardi Gras warehouse. The first edit to this sequence took out a two-second shot of Van Cleaf running through fire while shooting at Chance. A five-second chunk is removed from a scene, showing Chance shooting a man in a red shirt repeatedly, the bullets hitting in slow motion. The repeated shooting of a person seemed to bother the MPAA more than anything else in the movie, as this type of thing was excised several times. The next cut was a long one at eleven seconds during which Chance shoots two men wearing motorcycle helmets. He then utters the line "Give it a rest, pal." A four-second cut then removed a scene of a man dying with one of Uncle Duvet's arrows through his throat.

Another trim due to excessive gunfire cut the number of times Natasha shoots a man from six to three. There was a quick two-second cut of Chance doing a somersault, again probably for the flow of the sequence. There was another removal of repeated gunfire from Chance. A scene showing a bullet ripping through Uncle Duvet's knee was deemed unnecessary. A barrage of two-fisted gunfire that showed Chance shooting a man several times in slow motion was trimmed. Another three seconds were cut from that same scene when Chance kicks the man, then shoots him again. The final cut of this sequence was the removal of a five-minute close-up showing Chance shooting a man in the shoulder.

One curious bit of editing involved a simple scene in which Fouchon is sitting at a piano in his New Orleans mansion playing an aggressive piece by Bach. Woo intercut this with graphic scenes of wild African animals preying on one another. The effect has a sledge-hammer subtlety, but once again this kind of razzamatazz along with the several bits of slow motion, freeze framing and low-angled camera moves is pure Woo.

The studio cut yet another sequence, after the first preview, which surprisingly did not involve violence at all. It was something of a love scene between Chance and Natasha. After Natasha has found out about her father's death and Fouchon's thugs have beaten up Chance, they return to Chance's apartment where Natasha tends to his injuries. He pours out a story to her about how he never knew his parents and was raised by his uncle. The mood gets tender, candles are lit and Chance attempts to seduce her with a serious kiss. Natasha responds but then decides against taking things any further. The demise of this scene is rather unfortunate since it gave Chance some much-needed depth. The reason behind the cut is a good example of what happens when a studio takes the final edit of a film over from a filmmaker. It seems that some of the preview audience response cards indicated a level of disappointment that no skin was uncovered during the scene. Neither Butler's breasts nor Van Damme's oft-displayed rear end made an appearance to the chagrin of the sophisticated crowd. So, the studio reasoned, why show it at all?

Unfortunately, at this writing no un-cut or director's cut of the movie is available, but a bootleg copy of Woo's final version is out there in a poor-quality videocassette dub (the burned-in time code is an indicator that this was not meant for public viewing), available only from Internet video junkies.

One might expect that Woo would dip into his already-proven bag of tricks, using some of his Hong Kong movie moments to jazz up *Hard Target*. In fact, he only used one of his past sequences—he borrowed a scene from *Hard Boiled* where two opponents run along opposite sides of a wall blasting away through the wall at each other. The same sequence appeared in *Hard Target* when Van Damme and Vosloo shoot at one another through a wall in a warehouse. Woo describes the reasoning behind this self-pillaging: "I repeated that scene because I never really captured the sequence fully in *Hard Boiled*." He would repeat that very sequence again in *Face/Off*, with John Travolta and Nicolas Cage doing exactly the same thing. Woo, although seldom that self-reverential, is never above paying cinematic homage to one of his heroes. The opening fight scene in *Hard Target* is cut, scored and shot exactly like a showdown scene in a "spaghetti western" (*The Good, the Bad, and the Ugly* [1966]) made by one of his idols, Sergio Leone.

Producer Sam Raimi predicted that *Hard Target* would be "by far the best American action movie released in 1993." He was right.

Writer Georgia Brown made some interesting points about *Hard Target* in her August 31, 1993, review of the film in *The Village Voice*, "First—Woo didn't write it. In the second place it isn't really the film Woo shot because of the radical editing he was forced to do [and] then the studio allegedly did for him. Still, mercifully, it has his signature, even if smudged with some letters erased." Brown goes on to comment on the movie's style, "Though a dove flutters down at a crucial juncture, the essentials of a true Woo drama—passion, pieta, pathos—are missing. Even so, *Hard Target* has real style as well as terrific kinetic sequences, and I'll take it over all other summer pix any humid day."

Emanuel Levy echoes similar sentiments in his August 30, 1993, review in *Variety*: "John Woo, cult director of the new Hong Kong cinema, makes his eagerly awaited American debut with *Hard Target*, a briskly vigorous, occasionally brilliant actioner starring Jean-Claude Van Damme. However, hampered by a B-script with flat, standard characters, and subjected to repeated editing of violent sequences to win an R-rating, this pic doesn't bear the unique vision on display in Woo's recent hits *The Killer* and *Hard Boiled*." Levy goes on to state, "Ultimately, *Hard Target* is a compromised work, a stylistic hybrid of the American and Hong Kong action pics. But Woo's distinctiveness is still in evidence. He is a virtuoso at staging and editing intricate set pieces with precision, visual inventiveness, and humor."

Had Woo been allowed to release the movie he had made prior to all the cutting, it might have stood American audiences and critics on their ears, a seamless segue from *Hard Boiled*, his last Hong Kong movie, to his first American movie.

Hard Target made about $40 million in domestic box-office returns, which is respectable given that the movie was largely a disappointment to hard-core Woo fans.

Now that Woo had lived through his first Hollywood film and received an interesting education in Hollywood filmmaking, there was another lesson to come—the development process, known in Hollywood as "development hell."

After *Hard Target* performed respectably at the box office and got more than its share of ink, Woo and Chang decided to strike while the iron was hot, setting up their next couple of Hollywood movies. Woo had been stung by comments made by a studio executive that *Hard Target* looked like "a Chinese movie made in English." He vowed that his next movie would look every bit as Hollywood as a movie made by a director born in Hollywood.

Woo and Chang worked long and hard developing a movie called *Shadow War* for Sam Raimi's company at Universal Pictures. After pouring several months of work into the project it became plain that Universal had no real plans of making the movie. They moved on to another project that excited them. This one was called *Tear of the Sun*. Woo describes it, "We wanted to make an homage to *Treasure of the Sierra Madre* (1948), to John Huston." Chang recalls, "We spent eight months on it. We scouted locations around the world. But in the end we simply couldn't come up with the cast that the studio liked." They had been hoping to use Brad Pitt but the actor just couldn't fit it in since he had already committed to a number of projects.

The two partners were growing despondent when a firm "greenlighted project" offer came in from Twentieth Century Fox. It was a high-tech action movie called *Broken Arrow* and it was ready to go as soon as a suitable director could be found.

"It was sure easier to grab *Broken Arrow* than spend a couple of years developing something," says Woo. "And it was also a movie that would give me some experience with special effects."

Eight

1995–1996:
THE A-LIST

*"John Woo made it possible for us to bridge the
gap between Hollywood and Hong Kong."*
MICHELLE YEOH

In 1989, a nuclear submarine carrying atomic warheads
sank in the South Pacific. The warheads have never been
recovered. Less than a year later a B-1 bomber, also carrying atomic warheads, crashed in the Mediterranean.
Those warheads have also never been recovered.

Screenwriter Graham Yost based his screenplay *Broken
Arrow* on these two incidents. Yost had just scored big in
Hollywood when his previous screenplay, *Speed* (1994),
became an enormous hit both critically and financially.

Yost wrote the screenplay for *Broken Arrow* in much the same fashion as his *Speed* screenplay before it, to reflect his own tastes in movies. Yost explains, "I'd rather have fun with the genre than be heavy and brutal. I enjoy trying to think of everything that could possibly go wrong with characters in a given situation, and then try to come up with a clever way to get them out of the trouble I put them into."

Yost developed the screenplay with *Speed* producer Mark Gordon of the Mark Gordon Company, and executive producer Dwight Little, who may have also wanted to direct the script at one point given that he had directed the successful action movie *Passenger 57* (1992).

When Woo was approached with the script, he was looking for something to work on. Months of development work in Hollywood had left him anxious to get behind the camera again. This may have made the *Broken Arrow* script even more attractive to him. It was a "go" project. If he agreed, the movie would then go into active pre-production. He saw the script as a way to make a flat-out Hollywood movie, but still hoped to retool it to fit his own sensibilities.

But just before he signed to direct *Broken Arrow*, Woo received an intriguing offer from MGM. They asked if Woo would be interested in directing the seventeenth outing for Ian Fleming's James Bond, now being played by suave Irish actor Pierce Brosnan, called *Goldeneye* (1995). Woo considered it an honor to be asked but, with a healthy amount of trepidation, he decided to turn it down. "I was interested, I would love to see James Bond with two guns, but my James Bond certainly would not have been the James Bond they were expecting." The James Bond they got was directed by Martin Campbell and became one of the most successful films of the series. Within days of turning down *Goldeneye* Woo signed the contract to make *Broken Arrow* (1996).

Broken Arrow is about two crack Air Force pilots. Deakins (John Travolta) is a more experienced career aviator, while Hale (Christian Slater) is a young hotshot. Deakins and Hale are assigned to a training mission in the newest stealth bombers, which carry a frightening load of atomic warheads on board. It turns out that Deakins is an embittered traitor who plans to kill Hale, hijack the stealth bomber, then blackmail the government with the weapons that he has stolen. Hale manages to escape after ejecting from the stealth bomber before Deakins finishes him off.

Hale lands injured and disoriented in the desert and is found by a young deputy sheriff named Terry Carmichael (Samantha Mathis). Carmichael is highly suspicious of Hale's story until members of Deakins' covert militia comb the desert to find Hale. Now Hale and Carmichael are on the run together. They try first to tell the Air Force what has happened, and that Hale is still alive, then try to find the place where Deakins has stashed the weapons with the intention of disarming them.

Reviewers were divided in their opinions of *Broken Arrow*, some finding it a terrific American action movie, while others thought it silly, overwrought and just plain unbelievable. *Baltimore Sun* film critic Stephen Hunter had several interesting things to say about *Broken Arrow*. "With *Broken Arrow* the great Hong Kong filmmaker John Woo not merely becomes a full-fledged American director, but he finds a way to harness his remarkable dynamism and power to American storytelling traditions and cultural norms and all but re-invents the action thriller. . . . Woo is less a storyteller than a weaver of kinetic images, a man to whom the universe, far from seeming a stable arena in which to stage action, seems plastic, infinitely manipulable to be twisted and molded to his impulses, despite the laws of physics. . . . With *Broken Arrow* Woo ceases to be a cult filmmaker and we are richer for it."

A differing view of the film was provided by Roger Ebert. "One fundamental problem with the movie is that John Travolta is seriously miscast as a nuclear terrorist. Say what you will about the guy, he doesn't come across as a heavy. Watching this film, you understand why Dennis Hopper and Christopher Walken play so many mad bombers: because they can. . . . A lot of stuff gets blown up real good in *Broken Arrow*, including a train, four helicopters, and a mountain, but these brief flashes of special effects don't do much to speed up a slow, talky action thriller."

Travolta had never made an action movie before, even though he had been tempted a couple of times. He almost found himself in *Rambo: First Blood Part 2* (1985) but his part was eventually written out of the project altogether. Going into *Broken Arrow*, Travolta stated that it was a one-off project for him, and that he was not planning on doing another action movie in his life. Once he started working with Woo, however, he changed his mind and agreed to star in the even more-action-filled *Face/Off* (1997), Woo's next big-screen effort.

Originally Travolta was looking at *Broken Arrow* as a light picture that he could have fun with. "I think that audiences will enjoy this movie for what it is and I think they will be amused by what I did with the character of Deakins," says Travolta. He continues, "They've never seen me in this kind of character. In *Pulp Fiction* I played a misguided bad guy, but Vic Deakins is definitely more in the tradition of real evil." It was exactly this kind of anti-casting that led Woo to consider and ultimately cast Travolta in the main role of his movie. Woo remembers his thoughts at the time, "I enjoyed the contradiction between the real John Travolta, who has such a warm personality and an overall 'twinkle' about him, and the limitless menace of the character of Vic Deakins." Producer Mark Gordon, who previously produced *Speed*, concurred, "We wanted to try something different, rather than hiring someone who had played villainous roles before. We felt that it would really surprise the audience, both from a casting standpoint and from the point of view of seeing someone doing action stuff that you are not used to seeing. We want people to sit up and think, 'boy, I wasn't expecting that.'"

Travolta loves Woo and the feeling is mutual. Travolta was at one time a huge star, then a has-been, and then an even bigger star than he originally was—all within the space of twenty years. He first gained fame in 1975 on the hit sitcom *Welcome Back, Kotter* in which he played moronic, swaggering bully Vinnie Barbarino. A year later he appeared in Brian DePalma's hit film *Carrie*. Travolta received good reviews for his work in *Carrie* (1976) although he was playing little more than a big-screen version of Barbarino.

In 1977 he skyrocketed to global stardom when John Badham cast him in an urban drama called *Saturday Night Fever* (1977). The movie was an enormous hit, and the soundtrack album was even bigger, kicking off the disco phenomenon. Travolta took the role very seriously, shedding pounds and taking dancing lessons. The results earned him an Oscar nomination. He followed that with a safe choice, teaming with Olivia Newton-John in the movie musical *Grease* (1978). It was a huge summer hit and put Travolta on top of the movie world. His next choice would prove that no one, no matter how big a star, is bulletproof. His next movie was the truly awful *Moment*

By Moment (1978). This movie had Travolta as the younger man in an older-woman/younger-man relationship opposite Lily Tomlin. The movie bombed. He then accepted an offer from Paul Schrader to star as a male prostitute in *American Gigolo* (1980). Travolta developed cold feet when he started to think about his image, and he backed out at the last minute. Travolta then declined the lead role in the fabulous cop movie *Prince of the City* (1981), and his downward slide continued.

It took upstart filmmaker Quentin Tarantino to bring Travolta back into prominence when he cast him in his groundbreaking 1994 film *Pulp Fiction*. Tarantino was a huge fan of a little-seen film Travolta made in 1981 with Brian DePalma called *Blow Out* (Tarantino's praise of *Blow Out* has given it a new, and well-deserved, respect on video) and thought of no one else when writing the role of Vincent Vega.

The first meeting between Tarantino and Travolta consisted of the two playing the *Welcome Back, Kotter* board game. Travolta won. He accepted the role in *Pulp Fiction* and earned his second Academy Award nomination. The success of *Pulp Fiction* gave Travolta a whole new lease on his career and he scarcely took a breath before jumping into his next movie, and the next one, and the next one. Before long he went from making Screen Actors Guild minimum on *Pulp Fiction* to a reported $15 million plus for *Face/Off*.

• • •

Starring opposite Travolta was Christian Slater. Unlike Travolta, Slater had done some action movies in the past, but they didn't prepare him for *Broken Arrow*. "I tackled this role with all the intensity and preparation I could possibly come up with," says Slater. "It was like this was the role that I have been training for all my life."

Both Slater and Travolta saw *Broken Arrow* as an opportunity to extend their on-screen personas, and they were looking forward to working with Woo, especially Slater. "I'm a huge John Woo fan and I have been ever since I saw *The Killer* a few years ago."

Travolta admits that he wasn't familiar with Woo at all until Quentin Tarantino turned him on to Woo's movies when they were making *Pulp Fiction* together. Travolta took an armful of Woo movies home to screen them, and after seeing the *A Better Tomorrow* movies, *The Killer* and *Hard Boiled* he was intrigued and impressed. Travolta says, "John Woo's work in the action genre has a real sense of art to it, which is unusual. He is one of the few real artists delivering this kind of film."

Producer Bill Badalato was eager to put Woo at the helm of *Broken Arrow* because he sees Woo as a unique talent, and was one of the first to see that Woo's Hong Kong movies are admired not only for their action but also for the human emphasis he places on his characters. Badalato comments, "John Woo is a remarkable talent; he has an eerie quality about him. You know that if you just leave him alone, what he does will pay off in the end."

Although Woo was comfortable with his cast, and with the script, he was about to face a challenge that he hadn't met before in his moviemaking career—the use of special effects. "Computerized effects were something I really had no experience in at all, but since they are the wave of the future, I thought I had better start learning. When I learn, I like to learn from the very best," says Woo.

Woo indeed worked with, and learned from, the very best in the industry. His production designer, Holger Gross, previously designed the wildly ambitious Egyptian-influenced sets for *Stargate* (1994). Gross was now responsible for building a complete indoor mock-up of an abandoned copper mine that had been the site of an earlier location shoot in northern Arizona. The mock-up, snaking like a mounded mole tunnel across the floor, filled most of the entire airplane hangar-sized soundstage at the Twentieth Century Fox studios. It was made of wood and fiberglass, and was so well done that the walls truly looked like rock even when shown in extreme close-up. Several transport truckloads of the distinctly reddish earth from the Arizona desert were trucked in to lend even greater realism to the set.

This mine set was also equipped with a functioning freight elevator and an underground river. At a pivotal part of an action sequence in the movie Slater and Mathis use an underground chamber alongside the river to make a hasty retreat from imminent catastrophe. To make things even more difficult for Gross, the set had to be built with "fly-away" sections that could be silently removed and replaced even in the midst of shooting a scene, giving the always inventive Woo complete freedom of movement in close quarters. The result is classic Woo—a huge gun battle in a confined space where ricocheting and reverberation could cause all kinds of damage at any point.

Generally, Woo is not known for putting his actors in harm's way, knowing full well that an accident involving an actor performing a stunt that should really be done by a stunt person could jeopardize the entire movie. On *Broken Arrow*, however, there were a couple of exceptions to Woo's rule. The first involved the boxing sequence at the beginning of the film. In the scene, Travolta and Slater, who are friends but very competitive, square off in a boxing ring. Woo brought in former world boxing champion Carlos Palomino to train both Travolta and Slater so that they would be able to really box without the risk of getting hurt out of sheer ignorance of the sport.

The more frightening of the stunts handled by Slater concerned the scene where he is being dragged under a moving train. This sequence was shot during the latter stages of production on a forty-mile section of privately owned railway track near Livingston, Montana. The sequence, as written, involves Slater falling off the side of a moving train, being dragged along behind it, then pulling himself along underneath it. The scene is a variation on the same dangerous stunt performed in the classic John Ford western *Stagecoach* (1939). Stunt coordinator Gary Hymes remembers that "the whole thing was very scary for Christian, but the fact that he did it himself lent a lot of credibility to the scene. We had taken all the precautions necessary to make sure that nothing would go wrong, and it didn't." Slater remembers the day the sequence was shot with something of a shiver, "It was one of those times where I volunteered to do the stunt myself. I was actually insisting that I do it myself even though Woo said it was not being asked of me nor was I expected to do it myself. But then when the actual time came to shoot it I suddenly realized the enormity of the stunt. But it worked and I lived to tell about it."

For the scenes involving the "B3" stealth bomber, an imaginary adaptation of the current state-of-the-art B2 stealth bomber, Gross designed a craft that looked even more sleek and menacing than the original model. Since the stealth bomber is an ultra-secret military weapon that was designed and built in secret, the military was not prepared to cooperate with the production of this fictional recreation and enhancement. Gross and his visual-effects supervisor Don Baker used their imaginations to build a one-sixth scale miniature, one that measured eighteen feet long and fourteen feet wide.

The stealth-bomber sequences and many elements from the helicopter-chase and train-chase sequences were blue- and green-screen compositing tricks, a mixture of live-action footage and miniature props and computer animation. This kind of computerized moviemaking wizardry is something Woo remains uncomfortable with, but he lived up to the requirements of *Broken Arrow*. The special effects were less than satisfying, but since this was billed as a big Hollywood stunt and visual effects-filled movie, it drew in an action audience anyway.

Weapons expert Robert Galotti was brought in to handle the weapons and ammunition. Galotti had worked with Woo on *Hard Target* and would later join the crew of *Face/Off*. He is a decorated combat veteran who has seen action with the U.S. intervention in Grenada and the Desert Storm campaign. Known on the set as an "armorer," Galotti has the enviable reputation of producing huge pyrotechnics effects for action movies without ever having had an accident. In *Broken Arrow* Galotti arranged for over 60,000 rounds of ammo to be expended. Woo likes to assign each of his characters a personal gun, a gun that will be associated with only that character. It was up to Galotti to actually decide which weapon would be appropriate for each character based on their traits. Travolta's character, for example, carried a wooden-gripped Baretta machine gun, which is capable of firing up to 1,200 rounds a minute—a weapon that Galotti describes as being as elegant and deadly as Vic Deakins. Galotti built two sniper rifles for use in the movie that have a special sniper grip, stainless steel barrel, Red Mag, red-dot laser and the ultimate in night-vision scopes. The two sniper rifles designed specifically for *Broken Arrow*, each costing $24,000, are the only two such weapons in existence.

Variety film reviewer Todd McCarthy gave a decidedly mixed critique of the movie. "A virtual nonstop actioner that's heavy on imaginative destruction but light on coherence and character," writes McCarthy, *"Broken Arrow* doesn't score a direct hit but will still do the trick for thrill seeking audiences worldwide." He continued his overview of the movie, stating its "egregious continuity gaffs and pervasive implausibility push this closer to cartoon territory than was absolutely necessary." McCarthy adds, "John Woo drives the action at so ferocious a clip that his steering becomes more than a bit sloppy." McCarthy praised the performances by saying, "Travolta and Slater hold their own with the hardware and the scenery, delivering the kind of nifty star turns that this sort of vehicle needs." He saved his most singular praise for ex-football star and commentator turned actor Howie Long: "Howie Long looks completely at home in this rough context, acquitting himself perfectly well in his screen debut as one of the more sensible nasties."

Howie Long, who played the role of Kelly, is best known as one of the National Football League's most-honored and respected athletes. He played for the Oakland Raiders for an extraordinarily long 13 years and was invited to play in the Pro Bowl (all-star game) eight times. He is currently an analyst on the "Fox NFL Sunday" pre-game show. Long is a giant of a man with huge hands, and a neck three times the average size. He has an easy smile and a deep, friendly voice. He looks at his movie career with a pragmatic sense of humor. Long describes his early days on the set of *Broken Arrow*: "I went in to Twentieth Century Fox and they said that they were going to hire an acting coach for me. I guess they didn't know how I would take that so they went on to say that the acting coach was also for John Travolta and Christian Slater. I looked at the guy and thought to myself, 'John Travolta has been nominated for an Academy Award a couple of times, Christian Slater has been called one of the best young actors of his generation, and there's me.' I wonder who the coach is really for."

Woo, who was literally dwarfed by the towering Long, is a great supporter of the ex-footballer, as is co-star Travolta. Woo says, "I think Howie has great potential as a movie actor. He has a great sense of humor, a lot of natural charm and he is physically very impressive and imposing." Travolta, who shared a real rapport with Long off-screen, is even more supportive: "I think Howie can do this action movie stuff as a full-time thing—like Schwarzenegger or Van Damme. I'm rooting for him." A testament to the way Long was thought of by his new friends can be found in the early drafts of the *Broken Arrow* screenplay. In those earlier drafts Long's character was killed off much earlier than in the final version of the film. Travolta's prediction was either on the prophetic side or he actively threw his weight around to see to it that his new friend had yet another career. Shortly after the release of *Broken Arrow*, Twentieth Century Fox signed Howie Long to a starring role in their action film *Firestorm* (1997) about an elite group of super-firefighters.

Rounding out the impressive cast was Delroy Lindo. Lindo, a favorite actor of director Spike Lee, appeared in Lee's *Malcolm X* (1992), *Crooklyn* (1994) and *Clockers* (1995) and received impressive notices for his work in *Get Shorty* (1995) opposite Travolta. Woo fascinated Lindo, who had never heard of him before working under his direction in *Broken Arrow*. Lindo recalls, "I had not seen any of John's movies before I met with him to discuss *Broken Arrow*. But then as I investigated him I started to realize that there was this whole sub-culture of John Woo and Hong Kong action movie fans out there." When asked to consider how Woo looks at American culture and, more specifically, American action movies, Lindo thoughtfully responds, "You know, I think foreign-born directors have a more objective eye when they make movies in America or about America. I just finished a film with Scottish director Danny Boyle (*A Life Less Ordinary*

[1997]) and I once again enjoyed the purity of their vision. John thinks in terms of action, but not specifically in terms of violence. John's action scenes are always about something else other than violence."

Woo's feelings about *Broken Arrow* are complex. On one hand he says, "I'm very happy with *Broken Arrow*. It's not a perfect movie but I am still proud of it." But he has more negative feelings about his experiences with the studio brass. "Maybe I worked with some of the wrong people," says Woo. "Some producers started making problems for the movie. They tried to take it in their own direction. They made some changes without letting me in on it, which caused me to be quite confused. The other thing was that this was a pretty big special effects movie. We had spent so much time and money on those effects that there was no time left for the drama. All the drama scenes were shot in a hurry; sometimes I was getting 45 minutes to shoot a character scene. That was so unfair."

Once the movie was completed things didn't get any easier. "The editor and some of the producers were pretty old fashioned," recalls Woo. "They didn't like slow motion. They just wanted to cut the film the same way as *Speed* was cut. We didn't have time to fight hard for what we wanted."

Broken Arrow's release was the first time Woo received major criticism from the world press. Before this movie he was the cool new guy on the world cinema scene coming out of Hong Kong with guns blazing. When he made *Hard Target* the censorship angle could be used in his defence. With *Broken Arrow* Woo had made a movie that was offered to him, a "go" project that he hadn't really developed himself, and he was no longer being treated with kid gloves.

With *Broken Arrow*, Woo had made a $70 million Hollywood success. He brought the film in on time and on budget. He worked with Travolta, one of the biggest stars on earth, who came away from the experience saying, "I would work with John Woo again in a minute." Woo was now in a position to do pretty much anything he wanted to do—so he chose a low-budget remake of his 1991 Hong Kong film *Once A Thief* for Canadian television.

After making the pilot for *John Woo's Once A Thief* (1996) Woo said, "I fell in love with TV. Despite the tight schedule and a lot less money, I found that I can concentrate a lot better. Besides, I like working with a small group of people. In a movie, especially a Hollywood movie, there are so many people and always so much going on, there are so many distractions and politics and games . . . and meetings. It takes six months of meetings just to get the movie off the ground. I hate that way of working."

Woo gets even more descriptive when talking about the physical dynamics of making a movie for television. "Doing television is like warfare—you have to fight to make every second count. And I've learned that the people that work in TV work very hard and are very dedicated, they have great energy. They are like soldiers on a battlefield."

Taking a successful movie and turning it into a television series is not unusual. A series is established immediately by the association with the title of a successful movie. Recent examples include *Dangerous Minds*, based on the successful 1993 Michelle Pfeiffer film, and *Stargate*, taken from the popular 1994 science-fiction movie starring Kurt Russell.

Woo's challenge was to take a movie virtually unknown in North America and turn it into a television series. To his credit though, the plotline of *Once A Thief* is probably the only one of his movies that could be successfully translated into a weekly series.

Having a rising Hollywood star's name on a TV series was too much for Fox-TV to resist. Woo's Twentieth Century Fox feature *Broken Arrow* was doing steady business at the box office at the time. Since Woo himself would direct the pilot, the deal was sweeter still. So Woo went to Vancouver to make the two-hour pilot episode, but then Fox got cold feet and drew back to reconsider. Would people watch a series just for Woo's name? Fox decided to back out of the series altogether.

The entire project, including the pilot and the proposed twenty-two episodes to follow, was left hanging until Canadian production/distribution company Alliance

Entertainment stepped in. Alliance, with the help of the Canadian government-funding agency Telefilm Canada, propped up the series, breathing life into it. Since most of the twenty-two episodes of the series were already in the can, Alliance shopped them around to various broadcasters in Europe, and the show was bought instantly by several. The show then moved ahead with a solid $30 million, and a guarantee of a worldwide audience via the CTV television network in Canada, ProSieben in Germany, TF1 in France and broadcasters in Spain and Austria. Billboards and posters started popping up all over the place featuring the series' compelling moniker—*John Woo's Once A Thief—The art of action*.

Woo's name sold the series, but Canadian writers William Laurin and Glenn Davis actually came up with the episode ideas and wrote the scripts. Both Laurin and Davis have written for such American action series as *South Beach* (1996) and *Scene of the Crime* (1996). Both writers cringed at the thought of doing "just another action series." Laurin and Davis knew right away that what would set this show apart was a distinct irony, and humor. Davis says, *"Time* magazine, of all things, had the wisdom to say of the two-hour pilot movie, what you have to appreciate is that 'the whole thing is done with a wink', and once you get that, it all falls into place. You have to wink at the audience without overplaying your hand, but essentially what we're doing with the audience is saying, 'Isn't this fun?'"

Davis, a huge Woo fan, enjoys talking about the reasons for Woo's popularity around the world: "One of the reasons his movies just exploded the way they did is that, in addition to how brilliant they are, there's a slight cultural disconnection. There are differences between our culture and Hong Kong culture, which skews everything a little bit."

Laurin adds that this very popularity, that brand name if you will, enhances their responsibility as the writers for the show. "There is a brand and we take it very seriously and try to live up to it. When you look at John's films, especially the Hong Kong films, they are literally stunning. Part of our challenge is to produce television that leaves you with the same feeling. It's like going on the best ride at the amusement park. And that's what we are trying to do every week, without doing it via continual, vast action sequences, because, of course, that's impossible. The last four minutes of *Face/Off* were filmed over five weeks using six cameras a day. Well, in five weeks, we make three and a half episodes, so you're never going to have that result. You have to do it with other tools that are at your disposal in television—storytelling and character, and that's really what we spend our time doing."

The team of William Laurin and Glenn Davis is an odd one. They have been friends since childhood and writing/producing partners since as far back as either can remember. Davis remembers just how they ended up working with Woo on *John Woo's Once A Thief*. "We got a call from an agent at the William Morris Agency to meet John Woo just after he'd moved to Los Angeles from Hong Kong. John asked us what we had on our minds and we made up something on the spot without really knowing what he was looking for." Laurin adds, "I told him that we were light and romantic kind of guys and he smiled broadly and told us that that was just what he was looking for."

The series pilot stars Sandrine Holt, Ivan Sergei, Michael Wong and Robert Ito. They star as a family of master thieves who have been driven apart by jealousy. Two of the characters land on the right side of the law, and into the dubious care of someone known as "the Director" (Jennifer Dale). She heads up a super-secret law enforcement agency. They team up with a former cop (Nicholas Lea) and are assigned to bring down their former mentors and family members. Although it is odd to see the work of Woo on television, the style of the original pilot movie is quite evident. The plot of the pilot is filled with moral dilemmas and Woo's usual amount of gunfire, explosions and mesmerizing hand-to-hand combat.

Woo chose to shoot the pilot in Vancouver and insists that he did so because he wanted to, not because of financial restrictions. "*John Woo's Once A Thief* is a Canadian production. But I didn't shoot it in Canada because of the budget. The Hong Kong film business is slowing down for the obvious political reasons. Since 1990 I have wanted to work somewhere else—in Canada, America, England maybe. Vancouver is such a beautiful location, so similar to Hong Kong—the buildings, the lifestyle—and so many Hong Kong people live there that I feel like it is my home town." When asked about the TV pilot and how it compares to the big-screen version, he is quite open about the similarities. "It is pretty much the same story, and the action sequences are basically the same, but funnier. This time I focused more on the love story." Woo was intrigued by the prospect of television. "I have never worked in TV before so I thought it was worth a try just for the challenge of it. Then I thought that if the pilot became a series I could give jobs to a lot of young directors to come in and make the episodes."

Woo enjoyed the vigor of shooting for TV more than he had anticipated. "I made it in twenty-six days, that's pretty good, isn't it? Because, you know, it rained every day."

The television series allowed Woo to insert many references to other films. In just the first few episodes of *John Woo's Once A Thief*, references were made to such movies as *Bladerunner* (1982), *A Clockwork Orange* (1971) and *La Femme Nikita* (1991). There is even a bizarre reference to the seventies porn classic *Behind the Green Door* (1971).

In hindsight, Woo is quite open about the fact that he wasn't happy with the way that his original big-screen version of *Once A Thief* turned out, "Not enough time, not enough money, you know how it goes." When it was suggested that it might make fertile material for a television series, Woo had a rare opportunity to revisit the film and correct some of the things he was unhappy about.

The pilot for *John Woo's Once A Thief*, although not a very good movie, does have flashes of the wonderful humanity that Woo brings to his movies. Two examples from this TV movie illustrate that Woo is in a class of his own. The movie opens with a ballroom-dancing contest in Hong Kong. Woo films the scene with such lush stylization and choreography that it is really not much different than his action sequences. Woo used to be quite a ballroom dancer himself in his youth, and that exuberance comes through in full force. Later in the movie is a fight scene in a downtown penthouse that is signature Woo. But overall, there is a weakness in the casting, with the exception of the veteran actress Jennifer Dale as "the Director," that keeps the audience at a distance.

John Woo's Once A Thief was successful enough to be sold into syndication, probably on Woo's name alone. *Broken Arrow* made over $80 million domestically, and at least that again worldwide. It was an interesting year for Woo, a year filled with learning experiences and journeys down new paths. But things were about to get even better, as Woo was about to make a critical and financial smash and consolidate his position on the Hollywood A-list.

Nine

1997:
THE BIG YEAR

"I never look at a movie as being a big movie or a little movie or a feature or a TV movie—if my name is on the movie, I give it everything I've got."
JOHN WOO ON THE TORONTO SET OF *BLACKJACK*

As 1997 approached and 156 years of British sovereignty was coming to an end, Hong Kong filmmakers scrambled to consolidate and complete projects that were in the works. The films of Jackie Chan and John Woo were hugely successful in the foreign markets and both men were gaining worldwide popularity which caused shock waves in Hong Kong. Predictions of the fall of the prolific Hong Kong film industry were popping up everywhere.

The Hong Kong film industry is still the most potent in Asia but box-office receipts for Hong Kong movies fell to $750 million (HK dollars, approximately $99 million US) from $940 million HK the year before. Total admission for all films shown in Hong Kong were 14.2 million in 1996 compared to 20.2 million in 1994 and 33.6 million in 1993. Hong Kong remains a strong third behind the United States and India as the largest film-producing nations on earth. But a number of Hong Kong film industry heavyweights took their cue from Woo and Chan, and left Hong Kong to work in North America. Sammo Hung left Hong Kong to star in his own TV cop series set in L.A. (*Martial Law*). Kirk Wong and Ronnie Yu are making movies in America, as are Ringo Lam and Tsui Hark, although Lam and Hark have expressed serious intentions of returning to Hong Kong to support the film industry there.

With so much talent leaving to make movies in North America, the film exporting side of the Hong Kong industry suffered losses in the year leading up to repatriation.

But the historic shift in governments didn't faze all Hong Kong filmmakers. Some, like director Stanley Tong, state that "1997 was never an incentive for me one way or the other." Tong, director of the Jackie Chan crossover hit *Supercop* (1996), which was partially shot in mainland China, also made the jump to Hollywood. Tong said recently, "Forget 1997—the Hong Kong film industry would still have a problem even without it. The chance to

direct a film in America is an opportunity you simply cannot pass up, all political notions aside." The problems Tong
is alluding to are rooted in Chinese tradition. Says Tong,
"In mainland China, over 30 percent of the population is
uneducated. The Chinese culture, which we have stuck to
for so long, keeps the people from being open minded." If
the mainland Chinese ways are to be applied to Hong
Kong then the film industry will suffer greatly.

Woo is legendary for needing to keep busy all the
time. He always has to have not one, but several projects
on the go to feel content. In 1996 an aspiring director
named Patrick Leung, who had served as assistant to Woo
on several of his Hong Kong movies, wanted to make a
boxing drama called *Somebody Up There Likes Me*. When
he described his proposal to Woo, Woo stuck his neck out
and produced the movie for him. Woo is very cognizant
of the fact that he received many helping hands along his
trip to the top and he is often available to help those who
come to him for help.

John Woo had found a place in Hollywood. He could
be himself and make his movies without having to become
a Hollywood-type huckster. Now that he had found his
rhythm, he was about to move into high gear with
Face/Off (1997).

"'Make it bigger, do it quicker and make it better,' has
been our credo throughout the development and making
of *Face/Off*," describes producer Barrie Osborne. The $80

million movie would become one of the biggest hits of 1997 and would restore faith in Woo's ability to make a terrific action movie no matter which side of the Pacific Ocean he was working on.

To prepare for *Face/Off*, Woo's first Hong Kong-styled Hollywood movie, a project that was turned down by at least four other studios before finding a home at Paramount, Woo took another look at a movie with a similar theme that had fascinated him years before. That movie was the 1966 Paramount release from director John Frankenheimer, *Seconds*, in which Rock Hudson starred as a man who underwent radical plastic surgery to give himself a whole new identity.

Mike Werb and Michael Colleary wrote *Face/Off* as a speculative script. The writing partners had been wracking their brains, trying to come up with an action thriller, when they both went to a repertory theater on Hollywood Boulevard to catch a screening of the classic James Cagney movie *White Heat* (1949). The pair was intrigued by the idea of a police officer going under cover in a prison and not being able to get out. They took that idea, put a futuristic spin on it and came up with the high-tech, surgical identity switch. They had originally envisioned stars Sylvester Stallone and Arnold Schwarzenegger aping each other's well-known characteristics for two hours. Werb and Colleary wrote their first draft in 1990, neither of them having heard of or seen a Woo movie at the time, but coincidentally citing John Frankenheimer's *Seconds* as a major inspiration.

Set in San Francisco, the script contained none of the signature action that Woo would later add. The script was turned down several times (with Warner Bros. and New Line Cinema being among the non-takers). In 1992, Paramount Pictures bought the screenplay outright with recommendations that the science-fiction elements be toned down, and that the characters and the human-dilemma themes be strengthened. When Woo came aboard, he encouraged these recommendations to an even greater degree.

Before *Face/Off* was to become one of the smash hits of the summer of 1997, it would take seven years, two studios, three directors, fourteen producers and a couple of dozen studio executives, not to mention thirty separate drafts of the screenplay before it was ready for release.

Face/Off is a fascinating piece of speculative fiction that "contains enough plot for an entire series," as Roger Ebert wrote in his review. It concerns an FBI agent named Sean Archer (John Travolta) who is on a life-long hunt for a terrorist named Castor Troy (Nicolas Cage). Troy was responsible for the wounding of Archer and the death of Archer's son in a botched assassination attempt.

When Troy is apprehended he has threatened to blow up a famous Los Angeles landmark and kill scores of innocent people. Because he was put into a coma during his apprehension, and his brother Pollux has been sent to prison, Archer must find a way to get to Pollux to find the location of the explosive device. A bizarre undercover assignment is suggested involving the surgical removal of Troy's face, which will then be switched with the surgically removed face of Archer. With lasers Archer's body will be altered to resemble Troy's, and through a modification of the larynx, their voices will sound the same. Farfetched? Sure, but Woo does such a good job that we believe it.

Before Archer can successfully infiltrate the prison and connect with Pollux, Troy, who has remained faceless while in the coma, suddenly awakens. His associates come to his aid and kidnap the doctor responsible for the operations, forcing him to attach Archer's face to Troy's body so that Troy can exact revenge on his mortal enemy. Troy escapes and inhabits Archer's life (his family knows nothing of the particulars of the assignment) and gets close to his wife (Joan Allen) and his daughter (Dominique Swain) to use them as the ultimate weapon of revenge against Archer.

Archer is in Erehwon Prison (nowhere spelt backwards) as Troy trying to convince Pollux that he is indeed his brother. Archer ends up breaking out of prison when he finds out that the real Troy has awakened and is walking around in his body. The race towards a final explosive climax is what Woo fans had been waiting for since his arrival in Hollywood in 1993.

When it came to casting *Face/Off*, Woo thought immediately of Travolta. Woo and Travolta are kindred spirits. They are both a little old-fashioned when it comes to values. "John is my hero. He's a man with a great heart and he really cares about everybody and he's a man with no ego. He always tries to make everyone around him feel happy and he's very easy to work with."

Because of the nature of the two lead characters in *Face/Off* it was vitally important to Woo that he cast the Troy character with an actor that would be compatible with Travolta.

Woo explains, "We had to find someone else to match with John—not only physically match him but also be able to provide an equally interesting performance. John and I both like Nicolas Cage very much, because he also has a great heart and he really cared about everything we were doing. It turned out that they were a perfect match."

When asked about the degree of difficulty in achieving the mind-bending action sequences in *Face/Off*, Woo responds with a laugh. "They were all tough—the opening plane crash and the final speedboat chase. It was all very challenging and more dangerous than I would have liked. One of my stunt guys almost got killed during the speedboat sequence. He fell off the boat and grabbed the anchor chain that was supposed to keep him from falling into the water. He went down headfirst and banged his head against the side of the boat. He lost consciousness for a few seconds but managed to stay afloat."

Even with the advanced cinematic technology that pretty much allows filmmakers to fake anything in a seamless fashion, Woo still prefers the excitement that realism provides. "About 95 percent of the movie was the real thing—I've never liked miniatures and special-effects shots. Only a couple of the shots, like the boat flipping in the air and the surgery to remove the faces were special effects shots." And his actors, how did they feel about this preference for "the real thing"? "John and Nic had a lot of fun doing the action sequences because they had a lot of confidence in me and they know that I am pretty concerned about their safety, and they felt like they were dancers going through a dance routine. They were also confident that I would make them look good."

Dancing often comes up in conversations with Woo about his action sequences. "I view myself as a painter or a dancer. I like dancing. I just feel like I am doing a dance sequence when I am doing my movies. I am using musical theory to design my action sequences. I also like to show the visuals of the story as spectacularly as I can so they actually tell the story themselves. I hate long dialogue scenes. Every shot, every moment in my movies, is like a painting to me.

"When I was a kid I was fascinated by musicals like *Singin' in the Rain* (1952), *Seven Brides for Seven Brothers* (1954) and *West Side Story* (1961). They were my favorites.

All of my ideas for making action movies come from these movies. I care so much for the beauty of body movement, and the natural rhythm of general movement—it is very much like a musical."

Woo continued to have a hard time getting used to the corporate rigidity of big-budget Hollywood moviemaking. And the bigger the budget, the more suits that had to be answered to. Says Woo, "I never knew there were so many rules in Hollywood, you know, like the way the hero has to behave is rigidly set out. The hero has to be a straight person. He's got to be straightforward. He cannot shoot a guy with more than two bullets. I started to lose the fun of making a movie. The fun for me in making a movie is that you can do anything and everything according to your own feelings and imagination."

One of his trademarks, called into question during the making of *Face/Off*, was the double-fisted automatic handgun action. Woo cites classic movie influences: "John Wayne and the cowboys used two guns. In the old gangster movies they are holding one gun and they fire one shot. There is nothing visually exciting about that. I try to induce the feeling that the gunfire is sort of like a drumbeat. There is a rhythm to it."

During the filming of the escape from Erewhon Prison Woo had to confront one of his own fears. The scenes were shot on top of a 200-foot oil rig in the rough waters of the Pacific Ocean and involved Cage escaping the water-bound prison by dodging several hundred bullets from a helicopter gunship while throwing himself off the side into the churning water below.

Two problems arose. The first was that Cage is fearful of heights. "I was on top of this 200-foot-tall oil rig with no ledge to speak of. It was easily the most frightening day of my life, and I can say that without a hint of exaggeration." The second problem was that Woo is even more fearful of heights. Since Woo hates to rely on special effects and avoids them whenever possible, he would have to overcome his fear somehow to make the scene happen. Cage was willing to suffer along with his director for the sake of authenticity. Woo says, "If a character is supposed to be scared, I want to see those actors really scared. I have found that there is no quicker way to inspire fear in an actor than when his director is showing himself to be scared to death."

The prison-escape sequence is a pivotal moment in the movie and its set-up was extremely difficult. The scene was shot aboard a privately owned oil platform three miles off the coast of Queensland, Australia, in the Gulf of Carpenteria. Stunt director Brian Smrz took great care, and the stunt went off without a hitch the first time. Smrz comments, "I know Nic went through his own kind of hell on that day, but he really wasn't in any danger at all."

To represent the interior of this bizarre prison, an electrical power substation in Eagle Rock, California, was selected as a location. It came complete with twenty-five-foot-high ceilings and concrete walls that provided the dour atmosphere Woo was looking for. The floors of this fictitious prison are steel grids, and all the prisoners wear cumbersome steel boots that allow the guards to magnetically control their movements.

The job of creating these boots went to costume designer Ellen Mirojnick. She came up with a canvas diving boot with a brass toe and plate. One hundred and eighty pairs of these boots were constructed; each pair weighed over thirteen pounds. Mirojnick wanted her contribution to be every bit as meaningful and appropriate as the rest of the movie. "I wanted the boots to look like they could have been constructed in a prison metal shop—very elemental—so as to convey the idea of inmates building their own imprisonment."

Face/Off was shot almost entirely on location with a small portion of the movie being shot on the soundstages at the Paramount lot.

Production designer Neil Spisak supervised a team of illustrators, set designers, model builders and construction workers who created the physical settings in which FBI agent Archer and arch-criminal Troy find themselves. Spisak explains his task: "The two characters in the film are in a situation where they infiltrate each other's lives without anyone knowing. The look of the film has to reinforce the believability of this idea. The designs of the Archer home and office needed to mirror the stability of his life, so when Castor moves into them, entering the most intimate corners of Archer's life, we feel the frightening violation."

The other side of the coin is the prison environment in which Archer finds himself trapped. To visually convey the predicament, the set needed to be suffocating and assaulting to reflect those feelings of alienation. Spisak notes, "The idea is to show that both of the worlds are very real, but I was also faced with the challenge of keeping in mind that while designing these sets and these spaces I also had to make sure they were conducive to the action sequences. I had to make sure that John had enough room to move and create his mayhem."

It is a February morning in Los Angeles, Day 70 or so on the 105-day shoot. The scene involves Cage, dressed from head to toe in black and waving around a 9 mm mini Uzi machine gun. He is about to engage in a wild gunfight with his nemesis, played by Travolta, in a hall of mirrors. The 9 mm mini Uzi is one of the most powerful and destructive small weapons, but that's not what captivates director Woo. Woo abhors real violence, so the destructive power of the Uzi isn't really what he is thinking about as he lines up his shot. To Woo, the Uzi has a visual elegance. It is very small and compact, but has a powerful kick and emits an extremely bright flare when fired.

There is a noticeable tension on the set when big-action sequences are filmed. Too many things can go wrong. The crew now put protective earplugs in their ears. Cage himself wears small flesh-colored earplugs so the camera won't detect them.

Crew members closer to the action wear giant earphones that are similar to those worn by airport runway crews. The camera operators don goggles and make sure they have enough room to dodge flying debris. The call of "ten seconds!" goes out. Woo positions himself behind a monitor that is tucked far in the corner of the set. Because this scene involves explosives and precise timing of detonations Woo does not call for "action" in this scene. Due to the extraordinary precautions that must be taken around this much firepower, only a well-trained expert is allowed to give the signal for the scene to start. Again, that weapons expert is "Rock" Galotti, who has worked with Woo on all his American movies. This familiarity inspires confidence from both sides of the equation. "I know precisely what John Woo wants," says Galotti. "He needs a lot of weapons in his films. . . . He wants the characters to have distinct guns and he wants each gun to have a distinct sound."

Galotti examined the screenplay and carefully selected the weapons that would be carried and used by each character. Each FBI agent was equipped with SIG handguns,

MP-5 machine guns and the full stocked 9 mm subma-
chine gun MP-5A2. Galotti describes the selection
process: "The FBI weapons used in the film are used by
elite military and law-enforcement agencies in reality. For
the bad guys I selected weapons that are more commonly
available on the black market."

Cage steps into the center of the eight giant mirrors
that are set up around him. Travolta's double will scoot
around behind the mirrors while Cage fires at him with
the Uzi. Cage is given the cue—he starts firing the
weapon. The sound is absolutely deafening. You can feel
the roar within you, and that's just from the sound of the
gun. The demolition team now has to shatter the mirrors,
which have been implanted with explosive charges. After
a few minutes of the unbelievably loud noise, everything
is silent. Only the sharp smell of cordite hangs in the air.
Cage hands his weapon to the gun wrangler and strolls off
the stage having done his job.

At this point Cage has had a couple of years of staggering career success. He won an Oscar for his tortured
performance in the Mike Figgis movie *Leaving Las Vegas*
(1995) then went on to star in *Face/Off* and the summer
hit released a month prior, *Con-Air* (1997). When asked
about his decision to do *Face/Off* right after starring in
another huge action movie, Cage credits Woo. "The first
time I saw a couple of John Woo movies, it was like an
epiphany went off in my mind. The man had taken

violence and turned it into ballet. I know we've all heard that the movies of Sam Peckinpah were ballet-like but . . . John Woo approaches a level of operatic emotion. And somehow he did it in a way that didn't make me think 'body count.' I didn't feel that it was exploitation. It was so over the top that I felt I was watching comedy. The chance to work with Woo and be brought into that realm of his was too much to pass up. I was into this right off the bat."

The over-the-top bombast of which Cage speaks is demonstrated in one of the more visually breathtaking sequences in the movie. The scene involves a police raid on a hideout where Troy and his band of terrorists are holed up. Troy's four-year-old son is present during the shootout. Troy places stereo headphones over the boy's ears, and we see part of the gunfight through his eyes while listening to Judy Garland singing "Somewhere Over the Rainbow." Woo had been enchanted by *The Wizard of Oz* when he was a child in Hong Kong and wanted to include the song. However, the rights to use Judy Garland's version of "Somewhere Over the Rainbow" became hopelessly entangled in a legal challenge. The song remains in the finished film, but it was sung by Olivia Newton-John.

This exciting shootout scene was staged on the ninth and tenth floors of an empty building in downtown Los Angeles. With circular windows that overlook the urban skyline of the city, its massive scale and rooftop accessibility, Spisak and five-time Academy Award-nominated set decorator Garrett Lewis created a very lush, dramatic backdrop for Woo's breathtaking action sequence.

This loft shootout scene involved a truly staggering array of detailed preparations. Special-effects wizards Lawrence Cavanaugh and Bruce Steinheimer rigged the entire set, including the furniture and the walls, with over 5,000 bullet effects. These action movie veterans of effects were thrilled to be working with Woo because, as Steinheimer puts it, "John Woo knows what he can get, his visual scope is so huge that he is not afraid to ask for grandiose set pieces because he knows it is possible."

To add to the challenge, the decision was made to shoot this remarkable scene at night. Director of photography Oliver Wood wanted to ensure the lighting was up to the visuals that Woo had planned. Woo decided early on that this scene needed to be covered with multiple cameras, running simultaneously to catch the fluidity of the movements he had choreographed.

Producer Barrie Osborne relates that he often just sat back and marveled. "It really is great fun watching John Woo work, watching him conceptualize a scene, create the storyboards, anticipate the cuts in what he is capturing on film and use several cameras to create a visually compelling series of moments. No matter what he says, he really is the master of action," says Osborne.

As he did in *Once A Thief* and *The Killer*, Woo includes a wild shootout in a church near the end of the movie. He does this every chance he gets. "The church is a holy place," says Woo. "It's like heaven to me. So when I stage a gunfight in a church, it's to show that hate and war turn heaven into hell. People destroy all the purity and the peace. And this is the evil in the heroes, too. Sometimes they bring these things on themselves, and they have to die, too." Woo cracks a mischievous grin and adds, "It's just about the most blasphemous thing you can imagine, isn't it?"

Brian Smrz, a stuntman with twenty years of experience, was faced with the task of supervising a team of no less than fifty stunt people throughout the filming of *Face/Off*. Pyrotechnics everywhere, boats speeding through the water at over sixty miles per hour, jumps from great heights, and crashes galore were the challenges he faced. But Smrz was confident throughout the shoot. "He knows just where to put the actors who are part of the scene. That makes my job a lot easier. A lot of directors, especially the younger ones, simply say, 'I want this, I want that, give it to me now,' without realizing what goes into each of these scenes. That was never a problem on John Woo's set."

When asked about the relative merits of using stuntmen versus using computerized visual effects, producer Barrie Osborne is adamant in his support of Woo. "To take away John Woo's artistry and give it to a special visual-effects team would be a mistake. You want him in an arena in which he can perform his magic, and using stuntmen gives him the control he needs to accomplish that."

Face/Off opens with several police vehicles chasing a private jet, followed by a huge crash and then a spectacular gunfight. This sequence was shot at Southern California International Aviation, formerly George Air Force base. The airport willingly provided a crew and total access to the 10,000-foot runway for the sequence. Of course, Woo wanted the scenes to be as realistic as possible. That meant using full-sized planes instead of miniatures. One replica Jet Star jet was assembled from spare parts so it could be destroyed in the crash sequence. Another jet was placed on a trailer and driven up and down the runway for shooting interior scenes without a phony blue-screen effect to indicate movement behind the actors.

Face/Off ends with a truly spectacular speedboat chase. This sequence lasts about four minutes and contains more thrills than the entire movie *Speed 2: Cruise Control* (1997). The stunt work and logistics required were unprecedented.

The chase was shot at the Port of Los Angeles in San Pedro, one of the world's busiest ports. Locations manager Janice Polley and the second-unit locations manager Josh Silverman had their hands full. Because traffic through the port couldn't be stopped, and because tugboats, barges and other large ships cannot stop or turn quickly, elaborate communications systems had to be devised and utilized, which included the film crew, the port authorities, the coast guard, the port police, the fire department and the tugboat companies and their captains. One of the tugboat captains working on the movie, appropriately named Captain Waters, remembers that everything was set up with military precision. "Since shipping traffic could not even be impeded slightly, I was quite sure that what these *Face/Off* guys had planned would either not happen at all or would be altered significantly from the original plans that I saw. I was amazed that everything went off without a hitch. A new standard has been set with this movie where doing stunts on water is concerned."

In any movie, it's up to the actors to develop their characters, with input from the director and the screenplay. Cage's and Travolta's contributions to their characters were well suited to John Woo's style of moviemaking.

Take Cage for example. "Since most gangsters in movies are dressed in Armani suits," says Cage, "I wanted Castor Troy to have more of a mod look about him, I wanted him to look like the Liberace of crime. That was why I wanted him carrying gold-plated engraved guns." (The guns Cage is referring to are twin 24-carat-gold, .45 caliber handguns with custom-made dragon handgrips and cost reportedly $8,000 each.)

The identity switch in *Face/Off* is particularly entertaining. Travolta remembers, "I'd absorbed a lot of Nic watching him over the years. But I was interested in getting his permission to use some parts of him that I thought would be visually interesting. My version of Castor Troy's walk was a low-slung, sweeping kind of thing." Travolta asked Woo if he could apply this sauntering gait to Troy's speech pattern as well. "Nick slows down his speech and enunciates and pronunciates very consciously. His speech pattern is almost poetic."

Because Cage was held up on the set of *Con Air* longer than anticipated, he joined the production of *Face/Off* after Travolta had already been shooting for three weeks. The first thing Cage wanted to do was look at the scenes that had already been shot so he could get a sense of the rhythm and style of the movie. The first set of scenes was the opening sequence in which Archer's son is killed by sniper Troy's bullet.

Travolta remembers receiving a call from Cage right after he viewed the scene. "He called me up and said 'John, the gauntlet has fallen. I saw your scene and I wept.'" Then Cage saw the sequence Woo had cut to Louis Armstrong's "What a Wonderful World." Cage says, "I'm sitting there sobbing while I'm watching these sequences so I called John and told him that I simply couldn't thank him enough. He had made the decision for us about the level of acting that we were going for in the movie. I knew I really had to go to work."

Along with the action and high-quality acting turned in by Cage and Travolta, there was also a quietly solid performance turned in by Joan Allen, one of the finest actresses working in movies today. Allen has been nominated for Oscars twice, for her performance as Pat Nixon in Oliver Stone's *Nixon* (1995), and then again for her work opposite Daniel Day-Lewis in *The Crucible* (1996). Allen was enthusiastic about the movie because, "I got to do things on this movie that I have never gotten to do before. I had a gun to my head, I got to break chairs over people, this was real play acting at times but with an emotional core that was quite strong."

Travolta and Cage have nothing but praise for Allen. Cage says, "She is the anchor of the piece, the fulcrum whose incredibly precise reactions to this far-out circumstance make the situation real for everyone around her." Travolta is awed by Allen. "She has such weight and gravity as an actor. She balances Nic and I very well. She's the reality check in the movie."

For Allen, *Face/Off* also represented a jump to the big leagues in terms of salary; she was paid more for her work in *Face/Off* than in any previous movie. Travolta received in excess of $15 million for his work while Cage was paid between $6 and $7 million for his role.

Actress Gina Gershon, the sexy, tough moll, is a rarity in a Woo movie. She plays a character who is just as good with a machine gun as the male characters and can take and deliver a punch with equal aplomb. Gershon made a splash by being the only person to emerge unscathed from the breathtakingly horrible *Showgirls* (1995). She then gained some terrific notices for her bad-girl role in the indie-hit *Bound* (1996). Gershon was as surprised as anybody to be cast in *Face/Off*. "I'm a big fan of John Woo's and being that, I know he doesn't usually have women involved in the action stuff. So when the offer was made I said yes immediately. If you are going to do action, it is just as well you do it with John Woo." Gershon was also shocked by the person she met, after hearing the legend of Woo. "He's so gentle and his direction is so strange. He would tell me, 'Just make it more splendid' and, the funny thing was, I knew exactly what he was going for."

Woo chose veteran movie music composer Hans Zimmer to create the score for *Face/Off*. Woo wanted to go in another direction with the music, away from the standard action-genre music, towards a score with European influences. Zimmer, whose work includes the scores for such films as *The House of the Spirits* (1993), *Nine Months* (1995) and the Oscar-nominated score for *The Thin Red Line* (1998), remembers his early impressions of Woo: "His movies are so visually violent, but always driven by the themes of friendship, love and betrayal, all of which turn his shootouts into visual poetry. He is also the gentlest director I have ever worked with. He is very sensitive about what I am doing and paid me the high compliment of saying that watching *Face/Off* with my score laid in was like watching someone else's movie."

Face/Off is so crammed with stunts and action that many feared the movie would not make its release date of June 28, 1997. It would have been the second Paramount movie of the summer to blow its release date (the first being James Cameron's record-breaking epic *Titanic* (1997), which was scheduled for release on July 2 but was later re-scheduled to open December 19). The movie wrapped on April 1, but Woo is an efficient filmmaker, and when he is contracted to deliver a movie for release on a certain date, he delivers the movie on that date. On May 8 a half day of re-shooting had to be done, jeopardizing the tight schedule. The movie had undergone an early screening, and the resolution of the movie involving the orphaned son of Troy was deemed unsatisfactory and needed to be changed. Woo and Paramount had expressed conflicting views on how the movie was to end. Woo then argued with Paramount executives that the best route would be to shoot separate endings so that both would be available if the test screenings required an alteration. Paramount was sympathetic, but said the budget simply didn't allow that kind of luxury. Paramount previewed the movie and, according to comments on the audience response cards, 65 percent of the audience indicated they would prefer an ending that was more in line with what Woo and his writers had originally planned. That decision cost more than $300,000.

This aspect of Hollywood moviemaking bothers Woo to no end—this constant tinkering to try to, in a revisionist fashion, please as many audience members as possible. However, when all was said and done, "the ending the movie has now is the ending that I wanted all along." The fact that Paramount reversed their decision, allowing him to go back and re-shoot is indicative of the position that Woo now holds in the Hollywood hierarchy.

But the idea of re-jigging and toying with a film after it is completed still irks Woo. The experience Woo had on his first Hollywood movie (*Hard Target*) was so frustrating he wanted to head straight back to Hong Kong once it was finished. He still wonders about the relationship that filmmakers in Hollywood have with their audiences. He says, "Some people in Hollywood, they have a slight misunderstanding with the audience. They usually say that all the audience cares about is that the hero never dies and that the heroes should have no flaws. That the heroes never cry or have tears in their eyes. When I heard that I thought 'Wow, is that true?' I could hardly believe it." Woo feels differently about his audience. "I feel that all mankind has the same kind of heart, and they respond emotionally to things when you give them the chance."

Overall, Woo's dealings with the studio brass and the producers of *Face/Off* was a much more positive experience than his previous Hollywood films had been. Woo says, "Michael Douglas [the producer and movie star] was terrific, and the studio was very understanding. They let me do the things that I wanted to do and they weren't too upset when I wanted to make changes."

The size of American movies in general is still something that Woo is adjusting to slowly. "In America the scale is so big," remarks Woo. "If you try to change something at the last minute the people panic. In the opening scene in *Face/Off* we had John Travolta in a helicopter crashing into the tail of a plane. I shot it and thought, 'Well, this just isn't strong enough. I need it to be more powerful.' So I said, 'Hey! how about we blow up the engine?' The producer starts getting into some kind of panic. He's saying, 'Oh, John . . . that's going to take four more days to shoot.' I said, 'No, no. I'm going to do it because it's not been seen before.' So the crew and the stunt people were all very excited and they did it for me in just half a day."

Face/Off opened to across-the-board excellent critical response and enormous popular appeal. It made over $100 million in North America in its first six weeks. This success was widely attributed to the fact that finally a Hong Kong director was being allowed the freedom to make a movie in accordance with his own abilities and style. Marco Mueller, the director of the Locarno Film Festival in Switzerland and a frequent viewer of Hong Kong movies, said, "With *Face/Off*, the studio has let a Hong Kong filmmaker impose his signature on a Hollywood film. Hong Kong cinema has become an undeniable part of popular culture." The *New*

York Times, not often on the side of such studio fare, raved, "John Travolta is shockingly good in this thoroughly gripping film." Travolta was delighted: "With *Time*, *Newsweek*, and the *New York Times* and the *Los Angeles Times*, it was the first time ever in my career where I had 100 percent excellent reviews. *Pulp Fiction* didn't get that. Hell, I don't think *The Godfather* even got that. There are a lot of movies that get 85–90 percent positive reviews, but even to get to that level is quite extraordinary. This is unbelievable and it is all due to John's direction."

However, there were criticisms of Woo and his influence on North American cinema. Manohla Dargis wrote in the respected British film journal *Sight and Sound*, "But even as Woo's influence grows, his own work seems to have become not only less vital but less personal: as the Hollywood action film has become more Woo-like, the director himself seems increasingly less so." But even Dargis concedes that *Face/Off* is a triumph. "*Face/Off* does not lack in beauty of delirium: the film roils with gorgeous menace."

Empire magazine critic Adam Smith, in his rave review of the movie, wrote, "Woo's triumph, then, is to finally have realized the American-sized budget Hong Kong actioner. While *Broken Arrow* and *Hard Target* had moments of the director's inimitable style—essentially a willingness to use any and every filmic trick, especially his beloved slo-mo, *Face/Off* has Woo written through it like a stick of rock." But perhaps the critic that really captured the fun Woo injected into *Face/Off* was one of the most recognizable of movie reviewers, Roger Ebert. Ebert's review of *Face/Off* was entertaining and exact in its praise and examination. He wrote, "Woo and his writers find a terrific counterpoint to the action sequences: All through the movie, you find yourself reinterpreting every scene as you realize the 'other' character is 'really' playing it." Ebert went on to praise Woo by saying, "John Woo, who became famous for his Hong Kong action movies before hiring on in Hollywood, is a director overflowing with invention . . . the movie [*Face/Off*] is above all an action thriller, and the action sequences and the high-tech stuff are flawlessly done."

On September 25, 1997, Michael Weisbeth, President of Alliance Television, a division of Alliance Communications Corporation, announced that actor Dolph Lundgren had signed to star in a two-hour TV pilot called *Blackjack*, which would be shot in Toronto and directed by Woo. Lundgren played a character named Jack Devlin, an ex-U.S. Marshall who watched over people placed in the Witness Protection Program. After saving the life of casino owner Bobby Stern's precocious eight-year-old daughter Casey, Devlin is rewarded with enough money to live comfortably for the rest of his life in his Manhattan penthouse. But Devlin is pulled back into action when his friend and mentor Tom Hastings, the head of a top bodyguard service, is nearly killed protecting a beautiful young supermodel, Cinder James. As a favor to Hastings, Devlin investigates the shooting and finds himself competing with both Hastings' duplicitous team leader Tregesaar and Jack's deadly arch-enemy Rory, an ex-Marine sniper and Cinder's jealous ex-husband who is intent on killing Cinder. As Devlin skillfully tracks and defeats Rory, his life is further altered by the arrival of Casey, whose parents had named Devlin her legal guardian prior to their untimely death in an auto accident. Now a high-risk security expert, Devlin uses the latest technology to protect his clients.

It's a cool, clear evening in November 1997. The cast and crew of *Blackjack* assemble for an all-night shoot in a downtown Toronto warehouse. The scenes to be shot this evening include a fight scene between actors Lundgren and Phillip MacKenzie in a set that has been constructed to resemble a dairy warehouse. Lundgren's character has a terrible phobic reaction to the color white. Rory, played by MacKenzie, lures the unsuspecting Devlin into the warehouse for the confrontation because he knows the all-white environment will incapacitate Devlin.

As the crew sets up and the stuntmen ready themselves, producer Terence Chang strolls around the set checking on all the preparations. He is a tall man with an easy smile and a casual demeanor. Once everything is in place, Woo comes out of his trailer and heads into the warehouse for what will be at least twelve hours of work. He is a diminutive person to start with, but the numerous sweaters under a big parka make him look even smaller. Woo immediately discusses the main fight sequence with the stuntmen. He walks the stuntmen through the scene as he sees it. He wears a broad smile and watches with a precise eye. Lundgren appears, and watches quietly as the stuntmen go through their moves. Then he enters the set to ask questions and try out the moves.

Lundgren is a big man, approximately 6'5" tall with broad muscular shoulders. His thirty-eighth birthday was two days before, but you would not think him a day over twenty-five given the nature of his physique. Lundgren holds a master's degree in chemical engineering and can speak five languages fluently. He first came into prominence when he was cast as the Russian challenger to Sylvester Stallone's Rocky in *Rocky IV* (1985), a completely ridiculous movie that Lundgren managed to survive. He has since starred in several low-budget action movies, some of which are quite entertaining (check out *The Punisher* [1988]; *Showdown in Little Tokyo* [1991], in which he co-starred with Brandon Lee; *Red Scorpion* [1989]; and Roland Emmerich's *Universal Soldier* [1992]).

Lundgren's biggest asset is his awareness of his limitations as an actor. Contemporaries like Steven Seagal delude themselves into believing that they can do everything and play everything because they've been in a hit action film. Lundgren plays only characters he knows are within his range, and he does it well.

Bill Wong, the cinematographer, walks around the set checking the lighting for this scene, which involves a lot of bright white and coverage by at least four cameras, while Woo turns his attention to showing Lundgren the particular moves he wishes to see during the fight. It is quite a sight watching the very animated five-foot Woo demonstrating fight moves to the towering actor. The stuntmen continue to refine the fight as Woo coaches his actor. Something the stuntmen are doing catches Woo's eye. One stuntman has cracked Lundgren's stand-in behind the legs with a fake shotgun to bring him down. Woo takes the shotgun and animatedly demonstrates that he prefers to have the stuntman cracked in the back rather than behind the knees.

Woo is obviously not entirely comfortable with English yet and often gets his point across with gestures and pantomimes. As the rehearsal continues, it becomes obvious that Lundgren is uneasy with some of the physical dynamics of the scene. Lundgren is a martial artist himself, so he knows how to fight and he knows what will be easy to achieve, and what will be prohibitively difficult. Lundgren says of working with Woo, "He makes me look good. He takes what I do and adds to it what he does and it looks great. He hired me for a reason. If I live up to it then it will be a great time."

With all the necessary preparations done, the cameras are about to roll on the first part of the sequence. Lundgren rides into the frame on a beat-up dirt bike, stops, and reacts to all the white he sees. Everyone has been warned how loud this dirt bike will be, and earplugs were passed around. Woo, who is sitting behind the monitors in his director's chair, declines the ear protection with a smile, saying that he does not want them. When the bike starts up it is so loud it actually does cause Woo to flinch.

After a few tries that don't work because the bike is slipping sideways on the warehouse floor, the exhaust fumes become noticeable. Crew members pull shirts up to cover their noses. The back doors to the warehouse are thrown open for ventilation. Woo holds a handkerchief to his nose, until he finally gets the take he likes.

Woo then moves to direct a complex four-camera set-up of what most would consider a simple shot. It involves Lundgren astride the motorbike inside the warehouse, realizing that he has been lured in to an all-white environment. He gets dizzy, puts on the blue-tinted shades he always carries with him, draws a gun and climbs off the bike. Woo has this covered with an overhead camera, a handheld camera and two locked-down cameras, one positioned strategically behind large plastic vat-like containers filled with what appears to be milk. He strolls around the motorbike with his hands positioned like a camera viewfinder specifying what is to appear in the frames of all four cameras. He turns his attention to Lundgren and directs the facial expressions he wants during the upcoming scene.

Blackjack is unusual in that it is a TV pilot that may be turned into a TV series. It's Woo's first project since directing *Face/Off*, but you would never know it. He does not exude the attitude that comes from huge show-business success. The fact that he is directing something for television after a big-screen success is a rarity in itself. Most directors wouldn't dream of doing television after feature work. To Woo it is all work that he loves.

By the tenth day of the shooting schedule, everything is proceeding on budget, and according to plan. The set is now being flooded with atmospheric smoke, a dense, foggy substance, which gives the set the ominous, hazy look of a chilled environment.

Woo watches the material he has shot so far, playing it back on his monitors. The stuff is terrific. He then jumps up to join Billy Wong on the set, demonstrating the next scene so Wong can light it properly. On his way, Woo holds the 9 mm pistol that Lundgren will wield. When he plays out the scene for Wong he becomes Lundgren's character himself. Behind the camera Terence Chang is entertaining guests with stories of how Woo loves to do cameos in his movies and usually prefers to play a cop.

Two men, Mike Werb and Michael Colleary, writers of *Face/Off*, enter the set and are greeted warmly. Werb has just flown in from Amsterdam where he attended the Dutch premiere of *Face/Off*, and Colleary has flown in from Los Angeles. They are here in Toronto to meet with Woo about the just-completed second draft of the screenplay for *King's Ransom*.

Werb and Colleary stand and watch Woo work, both marveling at how such epics come out of this elegant little man. Both remark that Woo loves the process of shooting a movie. Even though he has been doing it for twenty years now, the magic has not worn off for him. They are both sure that Woo has already shot *King's Ransom* in his head several times.

Woo finishes on the set and returns to his monitors where he notices and enthusiastically greets Werb and Colleary. Woo turns his attention to his writers. Werb mentions that he has just read that *Face/Off* has gone over the $200 million mark in worldwide box-office returns.

Werb says, "Hopefully it [*King's Ransom*] will do $400 million." Woo is embarrassed and chides him, "You should not be so greedy. You should learn to be humble."

Woo is called back to the set just as a good-natured ribbing starts about John's rank in *Entertainment Weekly* magazine's 100 Most Powerful People in Hollywood survey (Woo is ranked 67).

It is 1:30 A.M. and shooting is about to start up again after a break for a midnight meal. Woo comes bounding back onto the set looking completely refreshed. He is asked to pose for some publicity stills before starting to work. He sheepishly agrees, then it is back to business. A big action scene is being set up, which involves shotgun blasts, gunfire and a vicious fistfight that is to take place in six inches of fake milk.

During the setup, Michael Colleary pulls up a chair beside Woo so he can tell him about the reaction to *Face/Off* at the recently held British premiere. Their discussion then moves to recent movies. Woo speaks of his dislike for *Air Force One* (1997) ("typical Hollywood movie with not enough story") and his love for *Shine* (1996) ("I cried at the end") and his curiosity about a little British movie called *The Full Monty* (1997) ("I'm working all the time now, but I will definitely go see it").

With the preparations almost complete, Woo dons his silly-looking black rubber rain boots to keep his feet dry against the milk flood.

It is almost 3:00 A.M. when Lundgren reacts to the call for "action!" He steps under a white pipe, which is exploded through special effects. Lundgren is drenched in white liquid. Before filming the big fight scene, Lundgren has his eyes flushed after getting some of the "milk" in them.

Woo checks the viewfinders of all four cameras, but something bothers him. There is too much clutter in the foreground. He calls for the set to be cleared. Once his instructions have been carried out, he stands looking at his empty set. There is nothing happening on the set at the moment, and no one is on it, but Woo studies it with a curious intensity. It is plain to see that the scene is playing itself out in his mind from every angle.

It is now 5:00 A.M. and this shooting day is still in full swing. Chang is still here even though he doesn't have to be. Chang, Woo and Wong engage in an animated discussion about the fight scene, and it is evident how much more comfortable Woo is when speaking in his own language. He seems to only let his guard down completely when he is with people he trusts and has known for a long time.

By 5:30 A.M. Woo has given the hulking Lundgren a comically animated demonstration of just how this fight scene should unfold. Woo has been working for twelve hours straight on this night, and there are at least another couple hours to go. He has not raised his voice once, nor shown any impatience, and he certainly has not chastised or berated any crew or cast member.

The fight scene is finally shot. It is a very rough physical altercation that has the two actors throwing each other around in the simulated milk. After the scene is shot a couple of times the actors are forced to change into dry costumes for subsequent takes

It is just past 6:00 A.M., and Woo is rehearsing Lundgren and MacKenzie on some changes that he has devised for the fight scene. As the actors go through the paces Woo claps his hands and says, "good, good" over and over.

Michael Colleary marvels at Woo's energy. He relates a story from the shooting of *Face/Off*. "The prison scene was shot in an old power station," says Colleary. "This was the dankest . . . place you can imagine and we shot there for three straight weeks. John remained calm and collected throughout it. Everyone got sick, virtually everyone except John. He did the whole fucking thing with a smile on his face."

The filming of the fight scene is not going well at all. Lundgren and MacKenzie are getting very tired, causing their moves to be off just enough to throw the entire sequence out of whack. Lundgren and Woo huddle to revise the fight. They shoot it one more time and it comes together perfectly. Woo then calls for the day's shooting to be wrapped. It is 7:10 A.M.

As Woo heads to his waiting car he smiles broadly and walks with a spring in his step. You just know he can't wait to get back on the set for the next day's work.

Ten

INFLUENCES

"The two things I'm most afraid of are accepting awards and talking in front of people."
JOHN WOO, UPON ACCEPTING THE 1997 MTV MOVIE
AWARD FOR BEST ACTION DIRECTOR

". . . Them Hong Kong movies came out, every nigga gotta have a .45. And they don't want one, they want two, cause nigga want to be 'The Killer.' What they don't know, and that movie don't tell you, is a .45 has a serious fuckin' jammin' problem. I always try and steer a customer towards a 9 mm. Damn near the same weapon, don't have half the jammin' problems. But some niggas out there, you can't tell them anything. They want a .45. The Killer had a .45, they want a .45." The preceding rant was uttered by actor

Samuel L. Jackson as Ordell Robbie in Quentin Tarantino's film *Jackie Brown*, which Tarantino scripted from the novel *Rum Punch* by Elmore Leonard. It is a testament to what Woo and his movies mean to popular culture. This reference to *The Killer* is pure Tarantino. No such reference exists in Leonard's novel.

The future of Hong Kong's movie business is still uncertain under Chinese rule. Hong Kong has, to date, derived very little income from China yet Chinese officials have made a fortune pirating Hong Kong movies for Chinese consumption. The repatriation could be the biggest bonanza the Hong Kong film industry has ever seen since they now might be allowed unrestricted access to the 1.2 billion people living in mainland China. Of course, it is entirely possible that China will place even harsher restrictions on the Hong Kong films allowed to enter their market simply as a way of protecting their own movie business in the years to come. Charles Hueng is one producer, however, who is betting on a windfall. A major player in the Hong Kong film industry, Hueng opened a 200,000-square-foot movie studio facility in Shenzhen in 1993 and has recently entered into agreements with the Chinese government that would allow him to build video stores and movie theaters throughout China.

When questioned about the future of Hong Kong films, Jackie Chan gives a surprisingly blunt answer. "It's a shame, I never watch Hong Kong movies anymore, because there are a lot of shit movies coming out right now. I don't like to say it, but I see Hong Kong movies as dying." That caution is shared by several of Chan's compatriots. Writer/director Wong Kar-wai says, "I think that the next eighteen months, after repatriation, will be the test period, for both sides. I think most of the filmmakers right now are thinking in the short term." Tsui Hark adds, "The major investors are starting to behave cautiously, some of them are pulling out of the industry altogether. The rest of them are just observing."

The investment issue aside, Woo's take on the change in sovereignty is somewhat optimistic. "People assume that censorship will be tighter, but I think it is only temporary. I can see China becoming more like Hong Kong. Since some of the filmmakers have left, it will leave more room for the young people and I think they'll create a new kind of Hong Kong movie."

To say that Woo has made it possible for other people involved in the Hong Kong film industry to take their chances in Hollywood is true. There have been other pioneers in film, Jackie Chan for instance, but Woo has blazed the trail for Hong Kong filmmakers to make mainstream Hollywood movies. While Chan is making huge strides in attracting crossover audiences for his truly spectacular films, he has yet to gain the acceptance that Woo has. Chan remains something of an oddity or a curiosity in the mainstream moviemaking world. Woo's contribution need only be measured by the number of other prominent Hong Kong filmmakers who have since been invited to Hollywood to make films. One notable example is Ringo Lam.

Lam has directed such Hong Kong hits as *Full Contact* (1992) and *City on Fire* (1987), the film that so much has been written about in connection to Quentin Tarantino's *Reservoir Dogs*. Lam's favorite movie is William Friedkin's seminal New York cops versus drug dealers seventies classic *The French Connection* (1971). It is quite evident that Lam is paying homage to Friedkin through *City on Fire*. Lam's *Wild Search* (1988) in which Chow Yun-Fat and Cherie Chung starred, had a plot strikingly similar to Peter Weir's 1985 film *Witness*. Lam was then invited to Hollywood to film *Maximum Risk* (1995), starring Jean-Claude Van Damme.

Like Woo, Lam has also had to learn some hard lessons about the making of movies in Hollywood today. Says Lam, "What I liked about *Maximum Risk* when I started was the idea of a man who has a brother that he does not know. That brother is killed. The surviving brother turns out to be the dead brother's dark side. In the original script the female lead (Natasha Henstridge's character), was much more complicated; she double-crossed Van Damme. This is what we shot. But after the first test screening, the studio did something that really pissed me off. They made me change her character from gray to white. They just wanted Van Damme to meet the girl, fuck the girl and everything turns out happy in the end. Happy ending. Bullshit."

Quentin Tarantino borrowed liberally from the plot of Ringo Lam's *City on Fire* when making his *Reservoir Dogs*. Of course, several Hong Kong filmmakers have practiced the same kind of borrowing from their Hollywood counterparts.

In 1993, the stuntman Vic Armstrong directed *Joshua Tree*, starring Dolph Lundgren. Armstrong openly admits that his garage shootout was based on Woo's in *Hard Boiled*. Armstrong had seen *Hard Boiled* at a festival and was so dazzled by it that he had to pay some kind of homage to it.

Actor Andy Lau has used others' work twice in his career, first with *Proud and Confident* (1988), which is almost scene-for-scene identical to Tony Scott's 1986 release *Top Gun* starring Tom Cruise. (The only difference was that the air force was replaced by high-intensity SWAT team training.) In 1990, Lau starred in *Crocodile Hunter*, in which he plays a SWAT team commander trapped in an office tower that is being controlled by escaped convicts. Sound familiar? It is an almost carbon copy of John McTiernan's 1988 Bruce Willis hit *Die Hard*. This perhaps proves the theory that there are really only eight original movie plots but a million different ways of telling them.

Although women are not usually strong characters in Woo's movies, he did include a few tough female characters in *Face/Off* and has been meeting with some heavyweight Hollywood actresses. "I met with Sharon Stone to talk about some projects. I'm sure she can play a very tough character with heart. We are now looking for just the right kind of material to work on together." Sigourney Weaver was so taken with Woo's style that she met with him and offered him a movie she is developing, which is based on a Japanese comic book.

The Chang/Woo juggernaut continues to roll through North American moviemaking. Woo is inevitably mentioned during discussions of influence on movies of the nineties.

When critics and film historians discuss the movies of the thirties they speak of *The Wizard of Oz* (1939) and *Gone With the Wind* (1939)—spectacles in color for the first time. In the forties movies were used as morale boosters during a catastrophic global war. The films of the fifties turned inward and were more reflective. Movies like *On The Waterfront* (1954) exposed people to realism. Cinema suddenly had a conscience. In the sixties movies reflected a time of upheaval in North America. A new morality and a distrust in "the system" was rampant in the movies. In a critics survey of the time, the counter-culture classic *Easy Rider* (1969) was voted as the movie of the decade, a decade that saw one of the grandest epics ever made—*Lawrence of Arabia* (1962). In the seventies the film-school philosophy took hold, and a crop of young filmmakers created a wave of stylish movies in which technique was as important as content. Terrific movies like *The French Connection* (1971), *The Godfather* (1972), *The Exorcist* (1973), *Chinatown* (1974), *Jaws* (1975), *One Flew Over The Cuckoo's Nest* (1975) and *Star Wars* (1977) also ushered in the era of box-office grosses as news items. *Jaws* saw to it that a movie needed to make $100 million at the box office to be considered a hit.

The eighties were a cinematic wasteland where excesses and consumerism in films such as *Heaven's Gate* (1980), *Dune* (1984) and *Ishtar* (1987) were reflected on the big screen. The decade kicked off with *Raging Bull* (1980), and most film historians say it ended there as well.

The nineties are an interesting blend of movies that were borrowed, remade, inspired by or paid homage to other movies and television shows. It has been a decade that has seen the cost of a movie rise to almost nonsensical new heights. In the nineties James Cameron spent $100 million, then $100 million plus, then $200 million plus, on individual movies. The nineties also saw the debut of Quentin Tarantino, hailed as the new voice in cinema, albeit one accented with the voices of many past directors. The nineties marked the era of the Hong Kong action movie. When filmmakers like Oliver Stone and Martin

Scorsese write fan letters to Hong Kong filmmaker John Woo, you know their influence is huge.

In 1998 Woo agreed to direct a television commercial for Nike. The commercial was shot over the Christmas holidays in the international airport in Rio de Janeiro and stars the Brazilian national soccer team. Romario, Ronaldo, Leonardo and Carlos Germano perform wild soccer stunts in the lineup waiting to be checked in for a flight to France for the 1998 World Cup. The spot aired in May 1998.

Woo is always animated when he discusses his future plans. Woo's upcoming projects are either locked down with financing and planning in place or being developed rapidly. He has often spoken with great enthusiasm and hope about a project called *The Romance of the Three Kingdoms*, an epic historical civil war adventure set in China 3,000 years ago. Woo describes the project as "the most ambitious dream for me. I have got to do that movie before I die." He has also expressed interest in making a western and, of course, a musical. When he describes his dream of making a musical, he refers to movies like *West Side Story* (1961), *Cabaret* (1972) and, strangely, Bob Fosse's dark, nihilistic 1979 masterpiece *All That Jazz*. Woo is now also considering the director's chair for the movie version of *Phantom of the Opera* (even though a legion of Andrew Lloyd Webber purists out there are actively petitioning against it). Style-over-substance director Joel Schumacher has also expressed interest in the project.

But the next Woo movie into the cinemas of the world will be the Tom Cruise film *Mission Impossible 2* . . . maybe. Woo had being developing his action/adventure/heist movie *King's Ransom* for months. He had made no secret of his admiration for Norman Jewison's *The Thomas Crown Affair* (1968) and was hoping to make *King's Ransom* in the manner of that film. But then MGM and United Artists announced that they would remake *The Thomas Crown Affair* with Pierce Brosnan in the Steve McQueen role for a summer 1999 release. This would force Woo to delay *King's Ransom*.

Because Woo needs to work constantly, he then began fielding offers from studios with projects that were ready to go. *Mission Impossible 2* provided the chance to work with Tom Cruise, an actor he admires greatly, so Woo signed on to direct.

Cast and crew assembled in Australia where *Mission Impossible 2* was to start shooting on March 5, 1999. In a dramatic move, Cruise, who also serves as producer on the film, suspended production for one month. Cruise was not happy with the screenplay and decided to lay off most of the cast and crew to re-tool the script. In April, 1999, the cast and crew reconvened in Australia with an updated script and new release date of May, 2000.

Is there a big picture to all of this? Probably. Young American directors like Quentin Tarantino and Robert

Rodriguez (*El Mariachi* [1992], *Desperado* [1995], *Four Rooms* [1995]) captured the attention and enthusiasm of a young generation. They were upfront about the movies that inspired them. Thanks to video, movies by, and the entire filmographies of, filmmakers from around the world are available for viewing anytime. These younger cinephiles then sought out Woo and were able to judge the originality—or lack thereof—of this new crop of American moviemakers. Woo helped touch off a new renaissance within the American movie industry, introducing a style that hasn't been seen since the end of the sixties.

Appendix

CHOW YUN-FAT

"I owe a lot to John Woo. He gave me the opportunity to become exactly the kind of actor I dreamed of becoming. It has been an honor serving as his alter ego."

CHOW YUN-FAT

Chow Yun-Fat is Woo's favorite leading man. Their work together has furthered both careers, and now when one is mentioned, the other naturally comes to mind. Through their numerous films Yun-Fat has become Woo's alter ego. He is the purveyor of Woo's bold, if somewhat naïve, brand of honor.

Yun-Fat was born on Lamma Island, a small island off Hong Kong's Victoria Harbour on May 18, 1955. His parents were farmers, and his boyhood home had no electricity. The hardships he faced were instrumental in forming today's diligent working habits. As a young boy, Yun-Fat sold dim sum by the roadside.

When Yun-Fat was ten, his family moved to Hong Kong, where he worked at a variety of jobs before responding to an ad for acting apprentices. He was accepted to Hong Kong's national TV training school and, in 1976, ended up in a series called *Hotel*, which earned him a tremendous following of loyal fans. He graduated to the big screen and sought diverse roles. Because Hong Kong's film industry is so prolific, many actors who gain popularity usually find it easier to simply play the same types of characters over and over again. Yun-Fat never did that. He tried his hand at comedy, romantic leads and action films in which he played both good and bad guys.

Yun-Fat prefers movies that are far from the action genre. He says, "Many of my favorite movies . . . are not the ones that are popular in the West. I much prefer movies like *Autumn's Tale* [1987] and *All About Ah Long* [1989]—I just love those movies."

Yun-Fat's first films earned him the equivalent of $400 per movie. He freely admits, "Those early movies were not successful at all—not with critics or with the audiences. They were lousy, let's face it."

At about this time Yun-Fat married Yu On-On, an

actor starring in a TV series on a rival network. The marriage was unhappy for both of them and ended quickly.

In 1981 Yun-Fat had a breakthrough. He made a movie called *The Story of Woo Viet* for director Ann Hui. Critics made note of the charismatic actor playing the Vietnamese boat person who becomes a killer out of desperation. The role allowed Yun-Fat to expand his range. The critics weren't the only ones to take notice.

In 1986, Woo wanted Yun-Fat to star in *A Better Tomorrow*, the movie that Woo had been planning for years. But the people in control of the finances were not convinced that Yun-Fat, whom they still saw as a lightweight actor, could pull off this ultra-cool, malevolent character. Yun-Fat wanted the part of Mark Gor because he understood that "John Woo was looking for someone who looked like a typical family man. But he can do all these things [shoot guns, kill gangsters] if he must, not like the typical Chinese kung-fu movie here."

Woo held out until he got his man. The success of *A Better Tomorrow* (1986) launched Yun-Fat to a new level and would make the Hong Kong gangster film genre an influential force in international cinema.

On starring in the *A Better Tomorrow* movies, Yun-Fat says, "I hoped it would do well so the boss could make money, but I never thought it would do that well. I enjoyed it while I was making it. I enjoyed the acting part, but no one was optimistic, right up to the finish of the film, even the boss at Golden Princess. But then at the premiere of the movie you can feel it in the atmosphere that the audience was very excited by the movie. There was shouting and clapping of hands, which is not something that happens in Hong Kong movies. I loved it."

Yun-Fat was disturbed that his character in *A Better Tomorrow* became a role model for young Hong Kong triad members. Asked about this while shooting *Hard Boiled* (1992), Yun-Fat replied, "Yes, that really did bother me, I was very concerned. So I told John Woo that with this film he would have to turn that around. I wanted *Hard Boiled* to be about a bond between policemen and try to make that a life just as heroic and appealing to the young people."

Yun-Fat is not as fond of the sequels that grew out of *A Better Tomorrow*. He thought they didn't live up to the promise of the original film. "John Woo was so excited after the release of the first one. With *Part II* [1987] I think he overdid it, out of control, out of his mind."

Yun-Fat remembers this film and its subsequent sequels with a smile. "My character died at the end of the first film, so when it came to do *A Better Tomorrow II* the only way they could get me back in it is to have me play my twin brother."

The role of gangster Mark Gor changed Yun-Fat's life profoundly. Even he was quite shocked by the results. "Before playing Mark Gor I made romantic comedies—

ever since then everyone likes to see me holding two guns and I don't know why."

When Yun-Fat and Woo were shooting the climactic gunfight at the end of *The Killer* (1989), Yun-Fat was cut badly, requiring stitches around his eyes. He was also injured during the shooting of *A Better Tomorrow II*. "In *A Better Tomorrow II* there is a scene where a grenade goes off in a house. The heat and the fire from the explosion actually knocked me out of the frame and set my hair on fire." This scene was included in the movie and the look of concern on Yun-Fat's face as his hair begins to smolder is clear.

Yun-Fat was also injured during the shooting of the New York scenes. For one shot he carries actor Dean Shek inside a darkened warehouse. "That was a tough shot. I was carrying him through the warehouse that was close to the waterfront, and there was a lot of water. I slipped and lost my balance and wrenched my back. It hurt so bad I couldn't move at all."

In 1988, Yun-Fat starred in seven movies and made uncredited cameo appearances in five others. Some were shot in as few as twenty to twenty-five days. When asked why he put himself through such a rigorous schedule he replies honestly, "I needed the money." His list of film credits growing, Yun-Fat's influence in Hong Kong movies is so dominant that when Hong Kong director King Hui approached Taiwanese investors, they asked, "Is there a role for Chow Yun-Fat?" When King Hui said that there wasn't, he was politely told to write a role for Yun-Fat or there would be no money to make the movie.

Yun-Fat cannot enter a restaurant in Asia without being mobbed. He shrugs this off. "Maybe it all happens because I was on TV all those years. The audience and I grew up together. They treat me like I'm a good friend." However, he finds that his star status can also mean nothing. "I remember once being arrested because I was going too fast on the freeway. The police officer knew who I was and asked me to give an autograph for his son, but he still gave me a ticket."

In 1995, Yun-Fat was yearning to get back to romantic adventure with a touch of comedy. He had made several very popular gangster movies with Woo and became a huge star in the process. But, as he had feared, audiences were close to reaching a Yun-Fat saturation point. Of his two hugely hyped movies made in 1994, *God of Gamblers' Returns* and *Treasure Hunt*, neither had earned even close to expectations. Yun-Fat decided to reinvent himself by writing the story for his next movie, *Peace Hotel*, himself.

Peace Hotel (1995) is set in Shanghai in 1920. A crazed lunatic, played by Yun-Fat, is on a killing spree. He wipes out an entire gang because he believes these criminals are planning to betray him, and because some of these gang members raped his girlfriend. After the massacre he turns the villa where the killing took place into a sanctuary for fugitives on the run.

The movie then jumps ahead ten years. The killer has successfully operated this place where criminals can live in peace until a new political boss (Lawrence Ng) viciously challenges the killer's safe haven when Yun-Fat's character gives refuge to a woman who has just killed a top triad boss.

Peace Hotel relies on a variety of influences. The movie looks and feels remarkably like a spaghetti western. Everything from the staging of the massacre to the plot line itself bears a striking resemblence to Sergio Corlucci's *Django* (1967). The main source of conflict in the movie is the woman who causes the safe house to be threatened. She is unlikable, even irredeemable, but still the hero protects her—also a spaghetti western mainstay. Even the musical score by Cagne Wong is highly reminiscent of legendary Ennio Morricone's score for *Django*.

Yun-Fat had desperately hoped that Woo would agree to direct the movie, but Woo was firmly entrenched in his new career in Hollywood. But as a loyal friend, Woo did agree to come to Hong Kong to oversee the film as producer. Yun-Fat settled for this "compromise," but it has been suggested that Woo did a lot more than simply oversee the production.

Many aspects of the movie lead one to believe Woo's hand was on the rudder here. Doves can be seen flitting wistfully through certain scenes. Slow-motion gunfights. Even the melancholy ballad that is played before the final big confrontation, all signature Woo-isms.

Peace Hotel is a terrific Hong Kong action movie with a solid performance by Yun-Fat. The call of Hollywood was louder and stronger, and he decided that now might be the time to consider making the leap. With the help of his manager Terence Chang, Yun-Fat actively sought a North American project, but it would be three years before he would sign to star in *The Replacement Killers* (1997), his Hollywood debut.

Yun-Fat, like Woo, is an avid fan of American movies and American movie actors. He lists Robert DeNiro, Al Pacino, Robert Duvall, Jack Lemmon and Jack Nicholson as his favorite actors. Yun-Fat considers Nicholson's performance in *One Flew Over The Cuckoo's Nest* (1975) to be the finest screen performance ever given.

Yun-Fat conducts himself with an ultra-cool demeanor that more than lives up to his onscreen persona. During the 1997 Toronto International Film Festival I met with Yun-Fat. He wore shiny black shoes, black slacks with a razor-sharp crease, a white shirt and dinner jacket. With his slicked-back hair, he looked like a Hong Kong James Bond. In spite of his huge popularity, he remains approachable and affable. There are places in the world where Yun-Fat cannot show his face in public without creating a mob scene. But still he remains a friendly man with a casual attitude towards what he does and what he has become.

Yun-Fat chatted comfortably about his work with Woo, and anything else I cared to throw at him, despite sometimes having to struggle with his English. He seemed to be trying to leave a good impression. The same was true of Jackie Chan when I spoke with him. Both were extremely successful men who felt somewhat inferior because they had not yet conquered the American market.

CHRIS HEARD: Are you concerned that people in North America know you only as an action star and know nothing of your comedic talents?

CHOW YUN-FAT: No, not at all—carrying two guns is one of my trademarks. And it is because I carry two guns in films that I now have had the opportunity to make my first American movie. We are talking about a market here that I have not really gained any kind of first-hand success in. It is a huge market.

I think it is obvious that most people who know anything about me at all know me from the John Woo movies that I have made. Maybe after *The Replacement Killers* has been released throughout North America, people will be comfortable with seeing me attempt other things. Maybe the studios will think of me when different scripts are being developed.

(This was to happen quickly; Yun-Fat went from *The Replacement Killers* to the Oliver Stone-produced *The Corruptor* (1999), and was expected to begin work opposite Jodie Foster in *Anna and the King*—a non-musical telling of the story of *The King and I* for Fox 2000 Pictures.)

C.H.: Did it come as a shock that audiences went nuts for you when you started doing action roles after the years you put in as a romantic, sometimes comic, actor?

C.Y.F.: Yes, absolutely. I spent fourteen years working in TV series, and I must have done over a thousand episodes. But it was always dramatic stuff, like a soap opera. I didn't really do much action stuff until 1986 when I got together with John Woo to make *A Better Tomorrow*. That movie was such a huge success throughout many markets where I wasn't really known. All those audiences had to go on was that performance. Filmmakers started thinking of me only in terms of that performance. Ever since then there have been very few romantic or comedy roles coming my way.

C.H.: Your work with Woo is quite celebrated, and has been compared to the collaborations of Robert DeNiro and Martin Scorsese or John Huston and

Humphrey Bogart. Do you have a special way of working together?

C.Y.F.: Well, we understand each other a lot. When we sit together to develop new stories or characters we often talk about the old movies that influenced us. Often we'll talk about movies in John's kitchen while we are cooking together. We both enjoy cooking and the happiness that can be found in the kitchen. When we are preparing something we compare it to a movie; all the elements of the movie become ingredients in the soup. It's a lot of fun.

(Woo's love of cooking and food is legendary. Most of his movie crews, actors and friends are treated by him at least once during each project. Just before making *Blackjack* (1998) Woo took the entire crew to a dinner at an exclusive Chinese restaurant. Before sitting down to dinner, Woo stood before the assembled crew and told them he would try to make them happy that they chose to work with him.

Glenn Davis remembers a similar event after the completion of 1997's *John Woo's Once A Thief* pilot in Vancouver. "After filming," remembers Davis, "John's other big passion is for food. When he finishes filming, he goes home and cooks a feast. And he is an expert Cantonese cook. When you go to dinner with him, he orchestrates dinner. It's just like one of his films. Just when you think it is over, more food arrives.")

C.H.: Will you and Woo work together again?

C.Y.F.: Absolutely, absolutely . . . in the future, hopefully the near future if it can be arranged. He is very busy with a lot of projects in North America, but we still talk often and keep each other up to date with what we are doing.

C.H.: Will it be different now that you have both worked in Hollywood?

C.Y.F.: There will only be one difference, just one.

C.H.: Which would be what?

C.Y.F.: The language.

C.H.: Has the language barrier been the most difficult thing to overcome in the transition to making Hollywood movies?

C.Y.F.: At the very beginning it was, yes. It was very hard for me at first. I had to take a lot of time to learn your language from scratch. I was like a kid in school. I had to learn grammar and phrases and I had to develop a vocabulary, and pay attention to pronunciation, everything. I had to learn tons of English words in very short order. I was suffering, let me tell you.

C.H.: *The Replacement Killers* is your first foray into Hollywood moviemaking but it certainly wasn't the first role in an American movie you've been offered. What made you choose this one?

C.Y.F.: My agent and manager were looking for scripts that didn't necessarily involve Chinatown gangsters. Before this, I was offered several American movies, but I was always the Chinese bad guy or the Chinatown mob boss. My agent and manager agreed that that wasn't the way to go for the first Hollywood movie, but I still had to do something that audiences would like and identify me with. As I said earlier, if this movie was a big success, then maybe the producers and filmmakers would offer me roles in things other than action movies.

C.H.: Is there something different about making movies in Hollywood than in Hong Kong?

C.Y.F.: The only thing that is different really is that moviemaking in Hollywood is so systematic. It is totally different in Hong Kong. In Hong Kong we can change the script and change the dialogue, even change the shooting schedule at any time. But in Hollywood everything has a very strict groove. Every day you have to complete a certain number of shots. There is very little changing of the dialogue.

Shot one is here, shot two is over there (his hand gestures indicate a rigid placement of the camera). Everything is very strict, which, when you are spending the kind of money on movies they spend over here, is a good thing really.

C.H.: The movies you made with Woo were very physical.

C.Y.F.: Yes, they sure were.

C.H.: Were they tough on you?

C.Y.F.: Not at all, not at all, because the difficult stunts were done by stuntmen. John Woo would not allow me to do anything remotely dangerous. A lead actor in a movie is very important because he's very expensive.

C.H.: Do you ever look at your surroundings and tell yourself how lucky you are?

C.Y.F.: Absolutely.

C.H.: Or do you consider yourself someone who has made the best of the opportunities that have come your way?

C.Y.F.: Both. Because some actors give better performances than me, have a lot more skill than I have, have better opportunities . . . but I am really lucky because I have always had the faith in the writers I've worked with and the filmmakers and actors that I have worked with and they have always done right by me. I feel that there are a few actors out there that are as lucky as I am. I've gotten really good roles all the time.

C.H.: As a kid growing up could you possibly have imagined all that has happened to you?

C.Y.F.: Not at all, not at all. Even today I have to keep myself grounded by telling myself that what I do as an actor, is just a job. Like your job, like anyone's job. It's not different.

C.H.: Do you consider what you do to be art?

C.Y.F.: No! No!

C.H.: It's a craft?

C.Y.F.: Yes, I'm a worker. Every day out on the set the director tells me where to go and what to do, and I do exactly as he tells me as many times as he tells me to do it without question. It's my job.

C.H.: Is that the difference between the way you do things and the way they are done in Hollywood, are the actors there too self-important, believing themselves to be artists?

C.Y.F.: For me it is simple, just obey your director and stick to what the screenplay says. Work.

C.H.: You are already quite well known throughout most of the world. Is it important that you crack the North American market?

C.Y.F.: Absolutely, absolutely! For me it has always been a fantasy to do a Hollywood movie. I have been an actor in Hong Kong for twenty-two years. People have gotten used to me, used to the kinds of performances I give. Now I am looking for a way to expand my talents and put myself in a market where I am hardly known at all. I think it is also good with Jackie Chan's movies doing so well in North America. He's a pioneer in opening up the North American market to Hong Kong moviemakers—

C.H.: Woo as well—

C.Y.F.: Sure, John Woo has been very important. Ringo Lam, Tsui Hark and now Kirk Wong has come over as well. We are all trying to make names for ourselves in the most difficult market there is to crack.

The genesis of any movie is usually an examination in lucky breaks, arranged chaos and forced manipulation of events. Antoine Fuqua, director of *The Replacement Killers*, was already a fan of Yun-Fat's, but he had no inkling that he would soon work with the actor when they were first introduced at a Christmas party thrown by Oliver Stone. (Stone is also a huge fan of Chow Yun-Fat. "Chow is a very honest and virtuous fellow," notes Stone. "He retains a sense of sincere humility, which is hard to do when everyone is telling you how great you are.")

Fuqua says, "I was impressed by his charisma, it was really bizarre. There were all these Hollywood people in the room when I first met him. In walks Chow, he breezes through the room like a sleek cat in an Armani suit and everyone was looking at him, saying 'that's Chow Yun-Fat' and for the rest of the time there I was doing the same thing—I couldn't take my eyes off the guy."

Several months later Fuqua was astounded and over-joyed when he was offered the chance to direct Chow in his first American movie. "I didn't even read the script. I said yes right away for no other reason than for the opportunity to work with Chow Yun-Fat," says Fuqua. "He walks into a room and dominates it without saying a word. He has presence. He is a lot like Clint Eastwood or Cary Grant in that respect."

When asked if he worried about *The Replacement Killers* being too closely linked to his Hong Kong charac-ters, Yun-Fat has this to say: "Actually, the character is a lot of fun. We tried to keep the dialogue down to a bare minimum, so the character is more like the ones Clint Eastwood plays. But what you really want to know is, did

I mind doing the same character that I have been playing for years now? The answer is, not at all, not at all. The studio paid me very well."

Yun-Fat's co-star, Mira Sorvino, spent over a year in Beijing studying Chinese history and literature and speaks fluent Mandarin. Ironically, Yun-Fat found himself in the strange position of co-starring with a young blonde American woman who could literally speak better Mandarin than he could. ("I was so embarrassed. She had all the Beijing slang and everything.")

During the shooting of the first action scene Yun-Fat aimed and fired with one hand. Producer Matt Baer and director Fuqua told him he should be holding his gun with two hands, in classic Hollywood-movie style. To practice, Yun-Fat explains, "The producers put me on a course at a ranch outside L.A. to shoot real bullets from real guns. This was the first time in my life that I ever fired a gun for real. It was powerful and quite scary." (Ironically, given the roles he's played, Yun-Fat hates guns.)

Yun-Fat's biggest obstacle was the language barrier. Much of the dialogue was trimmed from the original screenplay for *The Replacement Killers* to accommodate his limited English. Yun-Fat is open about his problems with English and the resulting frustrations. "I'm over forty, learning in school like this is hard for me." A dialect coach was hired to constantly push Yun-Fat and work with him on his lines. "Also, when I first came to L.A. I watched a lot of talk shows," says Yun-Fat, "Each guest talks slightly different so I was able to hear the subtle differences in American dialects." Mira Sorvino's fluency in Mandarin was a pleasant surprise and made life easier for Yun-Fat as he could communicate with her in Chinese when the English became too difficult.

Antoine Fuqua, when asked about Yun-Fat's behavior as compared to that of the American actors on the set, says, "You could see that it was a total change from what he was used to. There are a lot of boundaries and restrictions here that they simply ignore in Hong Kong cinema.

"Here we've got a lot of safety precautions that have to be seen to—it requires a whole lot of planning. In Hong Kong, however, they are a bit looser with that stuff. The scared looks on the actors' faces during the action scenes are real because the actors are actually scared to death."

A second difference had to do with union regulations. "In Hong Kong the crews work very closely together, everyone will do everyone else's job in a pinch, even Chow himself has done all that stuff." Chow found himself naturally doing anything on the set and getting into trouble for it. He hung around the set even when he wasn't scheduled to shoot. Fuqua remembers, "I had to follow him around saying, 'Chow, put that slate down,' 'Chow, don't push that dolly.' And he was actually quite taken aback by it. He would say, 'We're all making this movie together. We want a good movie and we don't have much time so we all have to help.' I had to tell the dude that every time he does that he risks having a grievance filed against him. He didn't really understand that—I still don't think he does."

Just before the cameras rolled Yun-Fat and his wife/business manager Jasmine stunned the entire production by arranging to take the entire cast and crew out for dinner—because "I pay them very high respects because they're the ones that make my dreams come true."

The Replacement Killers is a dark action thriller about a contract killer (Yun-Fat), owned by a powerful Hong Kong mob family, and his struggles to complete his contract and start a new life. As in all thrillers, he will have to fight his way out. It is a stylish, gorgeous action movie, and at a sparse eighty-eight minutes, certainly gets its point across in an economical fashion. But there is a major weakness with the movie; although Fuqua nailed the action stuff and obviously studied the Hong Kong action movies, he seemed to forget that the violent action comes as a secondary consideration to the broader story points of brotherhood, betrayal, honor and loyalty. However, Yun-Fat keeps his title as the world's coolest actor.

Of Yun-Fat's performance, Fuqua says, "It's a rare thing. You can see his soul in his face. Even when he is blasting away with a gun in each hand you feel right away that this guy is a new kind of movie hero, one that you can root for without hesitation or qualification." Mathew Baer, producer of *The Replacement Killers*, said, "This movie will be sold on the cool of Chow Yun-Fat."

Another 1997 release offered to Yun-Fat was the Twentieth Century Fox movie *Alien Resurrection* (1997). Chang recalls, "The writer of *Alien Resurrection*, Joss Whedon, is a big fan of Chow Yun-Fat so he wrote a draft of the script with a character especially written for him. But when I read the script I was furious. He [Yun-Fat] is in lots of scenes, but always in the background, carrying a big gun. Occasionally, he shoots some people. No way this is a part for Chow Yun-Fat."

After *The Replacement Killers*, Yun-Fat reported for work in February 1998 on *The Corruptor* for James Foley, director of *At Close Range* (1986) and *Glengarry Glen Ross* (1992). In this movie, Yun-Fat plays Nick Chen, a New York City police officer who, despite wanting to be a good cop, falls into corruption and violence after accepting the help of a Chinatown triad boss. Chen is partnered with a headstrong young cop named Danny Wallace (Mark Wahlberg) who genuinely wants to help clean up crime in Chinatown. However, Wallace also ends up falling prey to the seductive charms of the triad bosses. Both cops must fight to remain on the side of good. By the end of the movie, Chen has lost the fight and is killed, leaving Wallace to cover up evidence of Chen's corruption.

The Corruptor was developed by Oliver Stone, who also served as executive producer. He said that the movie was developed specifically for Yun-Fat after Terence Chang came up with the idea. "*The Corruptor* came to life after I read a magazine article about two corrupt cops in New York City. I immediately thought this would be a good vehicle for Chow Yun-Fat because it would give him the chance to play a corrupt, womanizing, street-wise cop. It is a lot like *Donnie Brasco* (1997) in that the tone of the film is very realistic."

Yun-Fat now resides in a lovely hillside home, designed by Frank Lloyd Wright, in Los Angeles and by all indications, he is here to stay. He loves California: "I have a lot of freedom here. I enjoy the food and the atmosphere. I enjoy the air here, it's better than Hong Kong. Mostly I enjoy hiking, it's kind of my hobby. Every Sunday I go for a two-hour hike; I prefer to go on the open side of the hills so I can have a view of the city and the ocean."

John Woo believes that his friend will succeed in Hollywood. "I have never been concerned that the American audiences will accept Chow Yun-Fat. The audience always likes something new, a new kind of hero. I'm sure that the audience will see that he is not just great at the action but he has a real heart and that will come through—because of that all sorts of people are going to be able to relate to him."

AFTERWORD

*"I never think about going back to work
on the same type of movies, I always want
to try for something new."*

JOHN WOO

John Woo has never learned to drive. He is especially
intimidated by the Hollywood freeway: "I don't think I
could concentrate on the road. I am so afraid on the free-
ways, even when I am the passenger."

Woo has settled into a comfortable life in Los Angeles
with his family. They live quietly, rarely appearing at
functions or other film-related affairs.

Martin Scorsese, after watching *Hard Boiled* (1992), wrote
John Woo a fan letter of sorts. The legendary director

wrote several questions about technique and camera posi-
tioning for the mind-bending action sequences in the
film. Woo was flabbergasted and completely tickled by
the letter since it was from one of his heroes. Woo wrote
back to Scorsese and told him that he got the ideas that he
needed to make his films from Scorsese's films.

Time will tell if Woo will be counted with the great
filmmakers like Kurosawa, Hawks, Ford, Scorsese and
Peckinpah. Woo is worthy of such consideration, but such
distinction is in no way guaranteed.

Consider the case of Victor Fleming, for example.
Most film fans will not know his name even though he
directed such movies as *Gone With the Wind* (1939) and
Woo's favorite, *The Wizard of Oz* (1939). His name went
largely unnoticed because he delivered solid movies, time
and time again, movies that were always more important
than the man who directed them. John Woo could also
fall into this category.

Woo's movies have a particular style—part Peckinpah,
part Melville and part Woo. Thanks to video it is now
possible to look at Woo's movies and the movies that
influenced him. Woo is like a great musical composer
who openly admits that his compositions are personal cel-
ebrations of all things that have moved him.

Hollywood rewards one thing and one thing only—
success. Woo has that. The global box-office sales of
Face/Off (1997) surpassed $300 million, meaning that

Woo, Terence Chang and Christopher Godsick could set up projects just about anywhere they pleased. Woo's next choices will determine his staying power.

Woo does belong on the same page with Martin Scorsese, John Huston and other filmmakers who are not afraid to make movies that travel straight from their hearts to the screen, and who are not afraid of risking big-time failure in pursuit of big-time success.

Most importantly, Woo loves the craft. "Every movie I make I try to make it better and better and I always like to give the audience a surprise. I like to challenge myself and not get too lazy. I want to find something new with each action sequence."

We will gladly wait to see where his vision will next take us.

FILMOGRAPHY

1971

Seven Blows of the Dragon <u>aka</u> All Men Are Brothers <u>aka</u> Seven Soldiers of Kung Fu <u>aka</u> Water Margin

DIRECTOR: Chang Cheh

ASSISTANT DIRECTOR: John Woo

CAST: David Chiang, Ti Lung, Chen Kuan Tai

1972

Killer From Shantung

DIRECTOR: Chang Cheh

ASSISTANT DIRECTOR: John Woo

CAST: Ching Li, David Chiang, Wang Chung

This film marked John Woo's first exposure to a large-scale movie that took the time and effort to develop interesting characters. Set on the eve of the Sino/Nippon War, it focuses on following the characters through their mundane daily lives as a cataclysm approaches.

1972
Four Assassins aka Marco Polo

DIRECTOR: Chang Cheh

ASSISTANT DIRECTOR: John Woo

CAST: Richard Harrison, Carter Wong, Alexander Fu Sheng

This movie tells the story of Marco Polo from the Chinese perspective, with action thrown in to keep the audience interested.

1973
Dynasty of Blood aka Chinese Vengeance aka Blood Brothers

DIRECTOR: Chang Cheh

ASSISTANT DIRECTOR: John Woo

CAST: David Chiang, Ti Lung, Li Hsui Hsien

1973
The Young Dragons

DIRECTOR: John Woo

1974
Games Gamblers Play

DIRECTOR: Michael Hui

PRODUCTION MANAGER: John Woo

CAST: Michael Hui, Sam Hui, Roy Chiao

1974

The Dragon Tamers <u>aka</u> The Belles of Taekwondo

DIRECTOR: John Woo

WRITER: John Woo

CAST: Carter Wong, Sammo Hung

1974

Hand of Death <u>aka</u> Shaolin Men <u>aka</u> Countdown to Kung Fu <u>aka</u> Strike of Death

DIRECTOR: John Woo

WRITER: John Woo

STUNT COORDINATOR: Sammo Hung

CAST: James Tien, Jackie Chan, Dorian Tan, Sammo Hung, John Woo

This movie is known for the combination of John Woo's direction and Jackie Chan's first big role as an actor in a popular movie. But it is strictly a kung-fu movie about yet another former Shaolin Temple student gone bad and a supreme fighter that is asked by the Shaolin monks to defend them. Jackie Chan plays a wandering youth and a pretty good fighter who is befriended by the hero.

1975

Princess Chang Ping

DIRECTOR: John Woo

A well-received film version of the popular Chinese opera. John Woo did a credible job of bringing this traditional-themed movie to the big screen and in doing so proved that he could handle large stories outside the pure action genre.

1976

The Private Eyes

DIRECTOR: Michael Hui

PRODUCTION DESIGNER: John Woo

CAST: Michael Hui, Sam Hui, Ricky Hui

John Woo helped out on this film as a favor to Michael Hui. This was the first film that featured all three of the popular Hui brothers and was an enormous hit.

1977

The Pilferer's Progress <u>aka</u> Money Crazy

DIRECTOR: John Woo

WRITER: John Woo

CAST: Ricky Hui, Richard Ng

This was the movie that put John Woo on the top of the comedy moviemaking genre. *Money Crazy* was a smash hit. Hui and Ng play two hustlers who try to help a young woman and her uncle recover some of the diamonds that were swindled from them by a crook. The whole movie consists of one attempt after another by the two to unsuccessfully steal back the diamonds.

1977

From Rags to Riches

DIRECTOR: John Woo

WRITER: John Woo

CAST: Ricky Hui, Johnny Koo, Richard Ng, John Woo (cameo)

This is one of the best comedies John Woo made and the one that helped to establish him as a comedy filmmaker. It is about a common man who hits the jackpot at the racetrack only to learn the same day that he is terminally ill. Finding it hard to cope with the fact that he is dying, he hires a killer to simply finish him off. He is then told by his doctor that the diagnosis was wrong and he is, in fact, not dying. With no way to intercept the hired killer, he is forced to go on a mad run for his life. Quite comical stuff.

1977
Follow the Star

DIRECTOR: John Woo

1977
The Contract

PRODUCTION DESIGNER: John Woo

1977
Hello, Late Homecomers

CO-DIRECTOR: John Woo

1977
Last Hurrah for Chivalry

DIRECTOR: John Woo

WRITER: John Woo

CAST: Wei Pei, Lee Hoi-San, Damian Lau

This is easily the best of the martial-arts movies John Woo made. The story line is dark and the action is violent. On his wedding day, a villain slaughters a man's family. He hires two mercenaries to exact revenge. They attack the villain's fortress and have to battle several martial-arts experts of various disciplines before getting to the guy they are after.

1981
Laughing Times

DIRECTOR: John Woo

CAST: Dean Shek

1981
To Hell With the Devil

DIRECTOR: John Woo

CAST: Michael Hui, John Woo

This was John Woo's variation on the Faust story about the spirit of a defrocked priest and a disciple of Satan struggling for the soul of a pop singer. Woo all but disowns this movie, yet allows that the special effects were better than they should have been given the way the rest of the movie turned out.

1982

Plain Jane to the Rescue

DIRECTOR: John Woo

CAST: Ricky Hui, Josephine Siao, Roman Tam,
    John Woo (cameo)

This is the only John Woo movie to date that features a woman as a lead character. A comedy about a homely woman (Josephine Siao) who is hired as an assistant to the owner of a giant Hong Kong business conglomerate. The entirely unlikable son of the conglomerate is kidnapped and the assistant enlists the help of a friend (Ricky Hui) to rescue the son with the hope of gaining favor with her boss. This movie is a comedy that really isn't funny at all. It vanished rather quickly.

1984

Time You Need a Friend

DIRECTOR: John Woo

CAST: Ren Ren, Shien Bien

This is a wonderful movie, easily the best movie John Woo made before rounding the corner with *A Better Tomorrow*. It's a Hong Kong variation on the theme of Neil Simon's *The Sunshine Boys*. It hits all the right notes and is beautifully performed and directed.

1985
Run, Tiger, Run

DIRECTOR: John Woo

CAST: Bin Bin, Pan Yin-Tze, Teddy Robin, Tsui Hark

This is perhaps the lamest, most ill-conceived movie in the career of John Woo. With the exception of the fact that this was the first time John Woo and his future producing partner Tsui Hark were ever professionally associated, this movie about a bratty kid trying to fit in with the lifestyle of his rich grandparents after the death of his natural parents has no real value at all.

1985
Super Citizen

PRODUCER: John Woo

1985
Love Lonely Flower

PRODUCER: John Woo

1986

Heroes Shed No Tears aka The Sunset Warrior

DIRECTOR: John Woo

WRITER: John Woo

CAST: Eddie Ko, Lam Ching, Chien Yuet San, Chau Sang

This tale of war and redemption isn't really a bad movie, it suffered from being made just before the groundbreaking *A Better Tomorrow*.

1986

A Better Tomorrow aka The Gangland Boss

PRODUCERS: Tsui Hark, John Woo

DIRECTOR: John Woo

WRITERS: John Woo, Chung Hing Kai, Suk Wah

CAST: Chow Yun-Fat, Ti Lung, Leslie Cheung,
    Emily Chu, John Woo

This is the movie that put John Woo, Tsui Hark and Chow Yun-Fat on the international cinematic map. This fascinating gangster movie, which deals with the internal and external existences of criminals, defines John Woo as a filmmaker.

1987
A Better Tomorrow II

PRODUCERS: Tsui Hark, John Woo

DIRECTOR: John Woo

WRITER: John Woo

CAST: Chow Yun-Fat, Dean Shek, Ti Lung, Leslie Cheung, Emily Chu

This reluctantly made sequel to the smash hit manages to be very entertaining and provides more action bang for the buck than its predecessor. The movie fuelled John Woo's moviemaking momentum. He was now a film-maker being called "important" in filmmaking circles all over the world.

1988
Starry Is the Night

DIRECTOR: Ann Hui

CAST: Brigitte Lin, George Lam, David Wu, John Woo

John Woo agreed to play a small role in this politically charged movie set against the backdrop of the Hong Kong student riots of 1967. Brigitte Lin plays a student who enters into an illicit affair with her married professor with rather melodramatic consequences.

1989
Just Heroes <u>aka</u> Tragic Heroes

EXECUTIVE PRODUCER: Chang Cheh

PRODUCER: Tsui Hark

DIRECTORS: John Woo, Wu Ma

CAST: Wu Ma, Danny Lee, Stephen Chiau, David Chiung,
Ti Lung (cameo)

Another do-a-favor-for-a-friend project from John Woo. The movie concerns rival gangs battling it out after a respected gang leader is killed. There is plenty of action but the movie goes nowhere due to a lack of real story or character development.

1989
The Killer

PRODUCER: Tsui Hark

DIRECTOR: John Woo

WRITER: John Woo

CAST: Chow Yun-Fat, Danny Lee, Shing Fui-On, Sally Yeh,
Chu Kong

The most famous Cantonese language movie ever made and one of John Woo's strongest statements to date.

1990
Bullet in the Head

PRODUCERS: John Woo, Terence Chang

DIRECTOR: John Woo

WRITER: John Woo

CAST: Tony Leung, Jackie Cheung, Waise Lee, Simon Yam, Chung Lam, Fennie Yuen, Yolinda Yan, Sam Yam Tat Wah, John Woo

This movie has been described as John Woo's *Deer Hunter*, which is a fairly accurate description. Thematically and visually similar to Michael Cimino's *Deer Hunter* (1978), it is also crammed full of Woo's ideas and views.

1990
Once A Thief

PRODUCER: Terence Chang

DIRECTOR: John Woo

WRITER: John Woo

CAST: Chow Yun-Fat, Leslie Cheung, Cherie Chung, Ken Tsang, John Woo

A heist film that allowed Woo to blend his prowess of a man of action with his previous incarnation as a deft comedy director.

1991
Rebel From China

CAST: (John Woo played a small role in this film as a favor)

1992
Hard Boiled <u>aka</u> Hot-Handed God of Cops <u>aka</u> Ruthless Supercop

PRODUCERS: Terence Chang, Linda Kuk

DIRECTOR: John Woo

WRITER: Barry Wong (based on an original story by John Woo)

CAST: Chow Yun-Fat, Tony Leung, Teresa Mo, Anthony Wong, Philip Kwok, Philip Chan, John Woo, Bowie Lam, Kuo Chui

John Woo's last Hong Kong movie to date is a spectacular action piece that has to be seen to be believed.

1992
Brother Versus Brother <u>aka</u> Double Dragon <u>aka</u> Twin Dragons

DIRECTORS: Tsui Hark, Ringo Lam

CAST: Jackie Chan, Maggie Cheung, Teddy Robbin, Nina Li Chi, John Woo

Jackie Chan plays twins separated at birth. John Woo played a small role as a priest named "John Wu."

1993
Hard Target

PRODUCERS: Jim Jacks, Sean Daniel, John Woo, Terence Chang

DIRECTOR: John Woo

WRITER: Chuck Pfarrer

CAST: Jean-Claude Van Damme, Yancy Butler,
Lance Henriksen, Wilford Brimley, Arnold Vosloo

John Woo's first film made in America for a major Hollywood studio (Universal) was filled with behind-the-scenes post-production problems but still ended up being widely regarded as the best American action movie released in 1993.

1995
Peace Hotel

PRODUCER: John Woo

DIRECTOR: Wai Ka-Fai

CAST: Chow Yun-Fat, Cecilia Yip, Wu Chien-Lien

This excellent movie was Chow Yun-Fat's last film before departing for Hollywood. A richly detailed movie in which Chow Yun-Fat plays a finely etched character known only as "The Killer."

1996
Broken Arrow

PRODUCERS: Terence Chang, John Woo

DIRECTOR: John Woo

WRITER: Graham Yost

CAST: John Travolta, Christian Slater, Samantha Mathis, Howie Long, Delroy Lindo

John Woo tries his hand at a big-budget, computer-and special-effects-driven American action movie. The results are spectacular, but not very memorable.

1996
Somebody Up There Likes Me

PRODUCER: John Woo

DIRECTOR: Patrick Leung

CAST: Aaron Kwok, Carmen Lee, Sammo Hung, Michael Tong, Hilary Tsui

John Woo lent his name and reputation to this movie, helping his former assistant Patrick Leung to make his directorial debut with this boxing drama that borrowed its title from the Paul Newman movie about the life of boxer Rocky Graziano.

1996
John Woo's Once A Thief (made for television)

PRODUCERS: John Woo, Terence Chang

DIRECTOR: John Woo

CAST: Sandrine Holt, Nicholas Lea, Ivan Sergei, Jennifer Dale, Michael Wong, Robert Ito

In a surprise move, John Woo makes a television version of one of his earlier movies. The end result of this homogenized version is not half of his 1990 Hong Kong film.

Woo and Chang then acted as executive producers for the weekly television series.

1997
Face/Off

PRODUCERS: John Woo, Terence Chang, Christopher Godsick, David Pessant, Barrie Osborne

DIRECTOR: John Woo

WRITERS: Mike Werb, Michael Colleary

CAST: John Travolta, Nicolas Cage, Joan Allen, Dominique Swain

John Woo's American breakout film. He demonstrates that a flat-out action-adventure movie could be made without sacrificing good performances, good writing and good storytelling.

1998
Blackjack (made for TV movie)

EXECUTIVE PRODUCERS: John Woo, Terence Chang,
Christopher Godsick

DIRECTOR: John Woo

WRITER: Peter Lance

CAST: Dolph Lundgren, Phillip MacKenzie, Saul Rubinek

John Woo improved on his first TV outing with this action movie about a troubled man who does heroic things reluctantly. Dolph Lundgren proves that he is a terrific action actor when working with a director of skill and vision. This movie would have been even better if Woo had been allowed to release his own version, which was edited without his participation.

1998
The Replacement Killers

EXECUTIVE PRODUCERS: John Woo, Terence Chang,
Christopher Godsick, Matthew Baer

PRODUCERS: Bernie Brillstein, Brad Grey

DIRECTOR: Antoine Fuqua

WRITER: Ken Sanzel

CAST: Chow Yun-Fat, Mira Sorvino, Michael Rooker,
Jurgen Prochnow

Yun-Fat's first Hollywood film. Fuqua gets the gunfights and the style, but he misses with the story line and the characterization. Yun-Fat came out looking cool and charismatic, but the movie is forgettable.

1998
The Big Hit

EXECUTIVE PRODUCERS: John Woo, Terence Chang

DIRECTOR: Kirk Wong

CAST: Mark Wahlberg, Lou Diamond Philips

Chang continues to use his skills to bring other Hong Kong filmmakers to Hollywood. Wong has made such high-octane Hong Kong movies as *Crime Story* (1993), *Gunmen* (1988), *Love to Kill*, and *Organized Crime and Triad Bureau* (1994). This movie is an action comedy that is full of razzle-dazzle but short on depth.

Upcoming

The following are films in various stages of development.

Mission Impossible 2

PRODUCERS: Tom Cruise, Paula Wagner

DIRECTOR: John Woo

WRITERS: William Goldman, Michael Tolkin

CAST: Tom Cruise, Ving Rhames, Dougray Scott

Sequel to the hugely successful 1995 action movie. This sequel was originally to be written and directed by Oliver Stone, but scheduling and creative differences saw Stone exit and Woo enter.

King's Ransom

PRODUCERS: John Woo, Terence Chang, Christopher Godsick

DIRECTOR: John Woo

WRITERS: Mike Werb, Michael Colleary

CAST: Chow Yun-Fat

This long-awaited movie reunites Woo and Yun-Fat in an action/heist movie with plenty of humor. Woo was inspired by Norman Jewison's 1968 film *The Thomas Crown Affair*. Woo has delayed plans for this film because of conflicts in schedules with Yun-Fat's film *Anna and the King*, and because MGM decided to remake *The Thomas Crown Affair* with Pierce Brosnan for release in the summer of 1999.

Windtalkers

PRODUCERS: John Woo, Terence Chang, Alison Rosenzweig, Traci Graham

DIRECTOR: John Woo

WRITERS: John Rice, Rich Batteer

CAST: TBA

During WWII a white GI is assigned to protect a Navajo Indian GI, whose native language is used as code in radio transmissions to confuse the Japanese.

A Chow Yun-Fat Filmography

1976:

THE REINCARNATION; LEARNED BRIDE THRICE FOOLS
    BRIDEGROOM MASSAGE GIRLS; THE HUNTER; THE
    BUTTERFLY AND THE CROCODILE

1977:

HOT BLOOD

1978:

THE PRIVATE LIVES; MISS "O"

1980:

JOY TO THE WORLD; SEE-BAR; POLICE SIR

1981:

EXECUTIONER; THE STORY OF WOO VIET

1982:

THE POSTMAN STRIKES BACK; THE HEADHUNTER

1983:

THE BUND; THE BUND PART II; BLOOD MONEY;
    THE LAST AFFAIR

1984:

LOVE IN THE FALLEN CITY; THE OCCUPANT;
    HONG KONG 1941

1985:

WOMEN; WHY ME?

1986:

ROSE; WITCH FROM NEPAL; DREAM LOVERS;
    THE MISSED DATE; 100 WAYS TO MURDER YOUR
    WIFE; THE LUNATICS; A BETTER TOMORROW; LOVE
    UNTO WASTE; THE SEVENTH CURSE; A HEARTY
    RESPONSE; MY WILL I WILL

1987:

CITY ON FIRE; TRAGIC HERO; SCARED STIFF; RICH AND
    FAMOUS; THE ROMANCING STAR; AN AUTUMN'S TALE;
    FLAMING BROTHERS; SPIRITUAL LOVE; PRISON ON
    FIRE; A BETTER TOMORROW II

1988:

THE EIGHTH HAPPINESS; FRACTURED FOLLIES; DIARY OF
    A BIG MAN; THE GREATEST LOVER; CHERRY
    BLOSSOMS; GOOD-BYE, HERO; CITY WAR

1989:

ALL ABOUT AH LUNG; WILD SEARCH; THE KILLER;
    TRIADS: THE INSIDE STORY; A BETTER TOMORROW
    III: LOVE AND DEATH IN SAIGON; GOD OF GAMBLERS

1990:

THE FUN, THE LOOK, AND THE TYCOON

1991:

ONCE A THIEF; PRISON ON FIRE II

1992:

NOW YOU SEE LOVE, NOW YOU DON'T; HARD BOILED;
    FULL CONTACT

1994:

TREASURE HUNT; GOD OF GAMBLERS' RETURNS

1995:

PEACE HOTEL

1997:

THE REPLACEMENT KILLERS

1999:

THE CORRUPTOR

SOURCES

Bouzereau, Laurent. *Ultra Violent Movies: From Sam Peckinpah to Quentin Tarantino*. Seacaucus, New Jersey: Citadel Press, 1996.

Chan, Jackie (with Jeff Yang). *I Am Jackie Chan: My Life in Action*. New York: Ballantine Publishing Group, 1998.

Danner, Fredric and Barry Long. *Hong Kong Babylon*. New York: Hyperion, Miramax Books, 1997.

Hammond, Stafan and Mike Wilkins. *Sex and Zen and a Bullet in the Head*. New York: Fireside Books (Simon & Shuster), 1996.

Logan, Bey. *Hong Kong Action Cinema*. New York: The Overlook Press, 1995.

Weisser, Thomas. *Asian Cult Cinema*. New York: Boulevard Books, 1997.

Magazines

Dargis, Manohla. "Do You Like John Woo?" *Sight and Sound*, September 1997.

Hampton, Howard. "Once Upon a Time in Hong Kong." *Film Comment*, July-August, 1997.

Harrison, Andrew. "The Beast." *The Face*, November 1997.

Howe, Rupert. "Doubles All Around." *Neon*, December 1997.

Kilday, Greg. "Hong Kong Goes Hollywood." *Entertainment Weekly*, July 1997.

Kulkarni, Neil. "Has Hollywood Tamed John Woo?" *Uncut: The Movie and Music Magazine*, November 1997.

Patterson, John. "Apocalypse Chow." *Neon*, July 1997.

INDEX

U

University of Oregon 110
Universal Soldier 189

V

Van Damme, Jean-Claude
57, 115-120, 127, 131,
200, 249
Vosloo, Arnold 117, 131, 249

W

Wages of Fear, The 32
Wahlberg, Mark 227, 253
Wan-Tho, Loke 12
Washington, Denzel 79
Way of the Dragon, The 29
Welcome Back, Kotter 142, 143
Werb, Mike 164, 192, 194,
195, 251, 254
We're Going to Eat You 36
West Side Story 5, 168
Where's Officer Tuba? 85
White Heat 164
Wild Bunch, The 32
Wizard of Oz, The 5, 175,
202, 232
Wong, Anthony 100, 248
Wong, Bill 189

Woo, John, birth of 2
early schooling 6-7
first film 18
marriage 31
move to Hollywood 110
makes TV film 155
Wong, Kirk 162
Wong, Raymond 33
Wu, David 70

Y

Yam, Simon 84
Yates, Peter 94
Yeoh, Michelle 111, 137
Yonghua Studios 12
Yost, Graham 137, 138, 250
Young Cop 86
Young Dragons, The 18-19,
21, 126, 238
Yuen, Fennie 83
Yun-Fat, Chow 43, 64, 72,
75, 98, 107, 127, 200,
207-229, 245, 246, 247,
248, 249, 252, 254, 255
Yu, Ronnie 162

Z

Zimmer, Hans 182

ALSO FROM LONE EAGLE PUBLISHING . . .

➤ **A CUT ABOVE: 50 FILM DIRECTORS**
TALK ABOUT THEIR CRAFT
by Michael Singer; Foreword by Leonard Maltin

Michael Singer takes the reader on an inside look at the
craft, art, passion and vision of 50 great film directors.
Candid, unrestrained converations weave a personal,
never-before-seen intimacy to each interview. This
collection of elite artists from Hollywood and around
the world elucidates significant developments in
filmmaking and sheds a surprising new light on
many familiar faces.
$19.95 ISBN 1-58065-000-7

➤ **THE ULTIMATE FILM FESTIVAL SURVIVAL GUIDE**
The Essential Companion for Filmmakers and Festival-Goers
by Chris Gore
$14.95 ISBN 1-58065-009-0

➤ **1001: A VIDEO ODYSSEY**
Movies to Watch for Your Every Mood
by Steve Tatham
$15.95 ISBN 1-58065-023-6

➤ **FILM DIRECTORS: A COMPLETE GUIDE (14th Edition)**
ompiled and edited by Lone Eagle Publishing
$90.00 ISBN 1-58065-019-8

➤ **FILM DIRECTING: KILLER STYLE & CUTTING-EDGE**
TECHNIQUE
by Renee Harmon
$22.95 ISBN 0-943728-91-6

➤ **SCHLOCK-O-RAMA: THE FILMS OF AL ADAMSON**
by David Konow
$19.95 ISBN 1-58065-001-5